Searching

Herbert Windolf

Searching

He who searches is not assured to find,
whatever it is that's on his mind.
But it is the path he trods which counts,
along which bits and pieces to be found,
not leaving the dedicated searcher blind.

The art of living well
and the art of dying well are one.
Epicurus

Reflections

Viewing past events
in the mirror of time,
the mind's eye conjuring
what today may yet rhyme,
while some incidents are forever burned
into the mind,
often good and bad intertwined.
Reflecting can mean
"looking back through the ages,"
but also to ponder insights, new,
to question their value,
how much they are true.
There's much to be learned,
while curiosity still yearns.

By three methods we may learn wisdom:
First, by reflection, which is noblest; Second, by imitation,
which is easiest; and third by experience,
which is the bitterest.
Confucius

Image

A whitewashed wall,
a stone-slab bench,
shared in the shade
with a long-time friend.
Pistachio shells at our feet
keep littering the sand.
We reminisce what all
has crossed our lives
and, still today,
occupies our minds.
Bougainvillea blooming
at our side,
a Mediterranean image
to delight.

The happiness of the bee and the dolphin is to exist.
For man it is to know that and to wonder at it.
Jacques Cousteau

3

Concrete

No, not the material
we use too much
to build and build
for all space to be filled.
Dredging lakes,
depleting beaches,
life there to be killed.
No, it is how most people think,
concrete their world is,
tangible, real.
Poetry and abstract thoughts
aren't their zeal.
If they only knew
that most of what they behold
is fiction, immaterial,
mind constructs,
since childhood told.

It is a folly for a man to pray to the gods
for that which he has the power to obtain by himself.
Epicurus

Girl,

together with "feminine" the only English term
into which is not embedded
"male" or "man."
It is an irritant to hear:
woman, mankind, female, humanity, humankind, and such,
where the feminine sex
is subjugated to the gender of male or man,
covertly saying that women are secondary,
don't count as much.
And do not mention the honorific "lady,"
a linguistic crutch.

Strength does not come from physical capacity.
It comes from an indomitable will.
Johann Wolfgang von Goethe

Woman

What is it that triggers my fascination
with a woman's features,
her face, her intelligence, her build, her grace
in real life or on TV?
There's the aesthetics, the beauty,
more often found in the young,
but also in the maturity
that age has brung.
Was it that I grew up with three stout women,
mother and grandmothers,
representing a different value,
that of perseverance?

Better a diamond with a flaw than a pebble without.
Confucius

Age

When we were young,
maybe seventeen, let's say,
we loved to tell our age-mates,
or whomever:
"I'm soon eighteen,
it's not far away."
These days, now at eighty-two,
I often hear myself say:
"I'm headed into my eighty-three."
A few decades turn us
three-hundred-sixty degrees.

Any intelligent fool can make things bigger and more complex . . .
It takes a touch of genius – and a lot of courage –
to move in the opposite direction.
Albert Einstein

Burst of Color

Yea, I have seen another year
since I last wrote about the burst of color
of flowering shrubs and trees,
which erupted in a surprising
shortness of days,
telling of spring
in its so beautiful ways.

The way to love anything is to realize
that it might be lost.
G. K. Chesterton

Appreciation

I ship and hand out a goodly three dozen
of volumes of my poetic prose.
Many recipients, I suppose,
will never look into the book.
Well, not everyone is inclined to read poetry,
even my down-to-earth verse,
being so disposed.
But there are three lady-friends, who,
in their personal way,
express their appreciation without delay.
One always looks forward
to the next book to come.
The other goes page by page
and comments on the poems
and the mottos she likes.
And the most verbal of them,
dare to even call me an inspired poet,
calls I don't deserve,
if I'm right.

What you really value is what you miss,
not what you have.
Jorge Luis Borges

Anecdotal

An account not necessarily true,
based on personal experience, belief,
not research or facts.
But many a man,
or woman, no less,
will utter such statements
for a point to make,
although it is most likely fake.

When you know a thing, to hold that you know it;
and when you do not know a thing,
to allow that you do not know it –
this is knowledge.
Confucius

The Art of Listening

and courtesy,
to let the speakers have their say,
the putting-aside of the desire to interrupt.
At the instant of interruption
the act of listening is lost
to the perception, the projection
of the no-longer-listener's thoughts,
with which he interprets, oft fallaciously,
the speaker's message.
Thus understanding fails.
Reading this
you may agree with this tale,
yet, the next time you enter into such a situation,
your ego will still run away
with miscommunication likely to prevail.
It requires years of training,
the will, the awareness, the self-control,
to acquire the Art of Listening,
if that be your goal.

I can feel guilty about the past. Apprehensive about the future,
but only in the present can I act.
The ability to be in the present moment is a major component
of mental wellness.
Abraham Maslow

The Long Way

Most people walk their life's way
as a matter of fact.
Things are as they are,
and they need to act,
to procure what they need
– at least so they think –
a car, food, a home,
a school for their kids,
and the many other things they think to miss.
No thoughts are spent on
the way we have come, as a species, that is,
through ages long.
What all we accomplished,
destroyed and beheld, hated and loved,
on the long path we tread,
pushed and shoved,
propelled and impelled,
and the long road ahead which
– if we are lucky –
we've yet to go.

Nature has placed mankind under the government
of two sovereign masters, pain and pleasure.
Jeremy Bentham

Privilege

It was in nineteen-fifty-six
when I rode a donkey to the Valley of Kings.
My buddy and I were the only ones there.
The French and Brits had attacked Egypt
after Nasser had nationalized the Suez Canal.
So all tourists had been evacuated by ship
to Khartum in Sudan.
The Aswan Dam was yet to come.
I marveled at the frescos in the
tombs of King Tut and Ramses the Great,
then at the magnificent temple
of Queen Hatshepsut,
a female pharaoh, quite rare.
All this without tourist mobs.
What a privilege it was!

People are to be taken in very small doses.
Ralph Waldo Emerson

13

Erosion

Granite boulders grace my yard,
rain, ice, snow, and heat
have pulled them apart.
With many I can reconstruct
how they once fitted together,
before time tore them asunder,
cracked and toppled them
into smaller parts.
Hundreds, thousands of years
it has taken to whittle them down,
ever smaller they will become.
And millions of years it will take
to grind them to sand.
Below them, still covered by soil,
others raise their heads,
awaiting their time
to become exposed and eroded
when I am long gone.

Yesterday is but today's memory,
tomorrow is today's dream.
Kahlil Gibran

Senior Sitter

of my friends
is what I've become,
taking care of the errors,
oversights, memory lapses,
just plain old age forgetfulness,
and then some.
Not to forget that I, too,
to the senior group belong.
But I'm glad
I still can take care of such things.
My mind is yet functioning,
while my body has ever more kinks.

One must always hope when one is desperate,
and doubt when one hopes.
Gustave Flaubert

Notre Dame

I wept for you "Our Lady,"
when I saw you up in flames.
Just as I did when I saw "Stori Most" destroyed,
the "Old Bridge" at Mostar in Bosnia.
Centuries-old aesthetic marvels, both.
I am not a Muslim, nor a Christian, nor a Frenchman,
but I cried for the loss, even if temporary,
of national symbols, world heritage, expressions of dedication
and human accomplishment to be restored, and preserved,
just like the war-damaged Cologne Cathedral was. -
During my year's stay in Paris in nineteen-sixty,
I climbed the stairs of one of Notre Dame's towers
a number of times.
Once, having entered the ticket vendor's room,
an American couple ahead of me,
their tickets purchased, were directed to a door
across the small room.
Opening it, they looked inside,
turned, and asked:
"No elevator?"

Many of those looking on as flames engulfed the building were in tears.
Their dismay is shared by believers and non-believers alike
in a nation where faith has long ceased to be a binding force.
From a BBC News Report

Visions

Both my visions are impaired.
My eyesight's getting ever more blurred.
The other vision,
what the future may bring,
is vacillating between a bright future
and a descent into hell.

Manus Manum Lavat

"One Hand Washes the Other,"
the Romans called it,
in English known as "reciprocity."
To give and take
for mutual benefit,
a most human trait.
It need not be a tit-for-tat,
a single tit would take care of it.
One-sided it can be,
but giving should never
be taken for granted,
for if it is, I beseech:
the taker might just become a leech!

The causes of events are ever more interesting
than the events themselves.
Marcus Tullius Cicero

Predictions

The future especially is hard to predict,
for the species that is,
not just the parochial United States.
In periods when things are not at their best
we tend to see the future poorly,
oft as a coming of the end of the world.
I cannot readily subscribe to this pessimistic spell.
But I'm torn between two scenarios:
A bright future,
or a descent into hell.

Life, if well lived, is long enough.
Lucius Annaeus Seneca

Tsunami

Lately a number of women have fled
the cunning, sorry Saudi state.
I wish for it to become a tsunami
to bring, sooner than later,
the end to this medieval, religious estate.

Under a government, which imprisons any unjustly,
the true place for a just man is also a prison.
Henry David Thoreau

20

There was a Time

I, Australopithecus,
three million years ago,
walked erect, like my hominin descendents,
but with a brain of only 450 cc,
not larger than my future relative,
a chimpanzee.
Not yet having learned to tend a fire,
I, and my family
must still spend the night in trees,
for there are carnivores
preying on my mate,
my children, and me.

He who has overcome his fears will truly be free.
Aristotle

Pipsqueak

Watching the movie, Apollo 13, once more,
only then, belatedly, did I fully realize
what these three guys,
Lovell, Haise, and Swigert, went through
in 1970, out in space,
in their crippled spacecraft,
not knowing what their fate would be.
Thus, when I teased Jim Lovell over dinner,
saying that Tom Hanks, portraying Lovell,
had done a better job bringing Apollo 13 back,
it occurred to me
what a pipsqueak I had been.

Nothing in life is to be feared,
it is only to be understood.
Marie Curie

Groping

For thousands of years
we have been groping our way,
from the morass of ignorance
to today's slightly more enlightened way.
Most people do live day by day,
ignorant of, or not caring
how we got to where we are today.
Classical Greeks thought the world consisted
of earth, air, water and fire.
What all they missed!
From Not Knowing,
it was hard to discern
what the world consisted of,
nature's secrets to discover and to learn.
But once enough data accumulated,
the ancients arrived at a paradigm
from which to explore further
through years of time.
Thus we keep exploring nature, the universe
by ever new paradigms.

Everything should be made as simple as possible,
but not simpler.
Albert Einstein

William of Ockham

A Franciscan friar, back in the 14th century,
made the astute, the logical observation
that "less can be more,"
also known as "the law of briefness,"
of parsimony.
The fewer data explaining a guess,
the greater the likelihood of explanatory success.
But if the simpler explanation
is equal to the complex one,
then use the latter without it being overdone.
This far back go our attempts
at understanding our world.
Ever since, the above observation
as "Occam's Razor" is beheld.

Is God willing to prevent evil, but not able?
Then he is not omnipotent.
Is he able, but not willing?
Then he is malevolent.
Is he both able and willing?
Then whence cometh evil?
Is he neither able nor willing?
Then why call him God?
Epicurus, 33 A.D.

Playing with Words

To play with words my forté is.
Yet it evolved only
through the past twenty-five years.
Through my plentiful writings
I acquired the English vocabulary
to concoct double-meanings,
to think outside the box
and by this to tease.
Yet I recall that already in my early twenties
I was egged-on
to apply my word-smithing in German
to tease a third party.
If done with women it is often called flirting.
With men it is – what?
Being hetero, my drift is certain.
In essence it is for amusement,
not a serious action for someone's attraction,
never aggressive, sometimes insinuative,
usually innocent,
if only to enjoy life in lively communication.

Our deeds follow us, and what we have been
makes us what we are.
John Dykes

The Wheel

Some things are material, others ethereal.
I have assigned them positions on a wheel.
The material ones, like a desk, a house, a club,
have found their place close to the hub.
Then there are clouds, the makeup of air,
the chemistry of water, radiating from the axis.
They have less substance, cannot be directly perceived,
but nevertheless are there.
The farther I travel along the spokes,
getting closer to the rim,
that's where I've located things like
supernovae, quantum mechanics,
$E = mc2$, and the Big Bang,
or what was produced by Max Planck.
Outside the rim there are things esoteric,
like dark matter, dark energy, black holes, and such.
And even farther out are found
a creating entity, elves, and a soul,
or other fictional concoctions,
mind-produced, mind-boggling options.

It is a very sad thing that nowadays
there is so little useless information around.
Oscar Wilde

Upheaval

Through the ages
cultures are periodically turned upside down.
The causes may be societal, economic, political, or war.
Some cultures crash or fade away.
Others revive to see another day.
Every few decades, we in the West,
have encountered such upsets,
overcoming the various threats,
to see our conditions improved and reset.
This is what upheavals can be about,
a reset to new shores,
from old patterns to break out,
a renewal, improvement,
from what has been.
Thus, when in doubt, in gloom and distress,
remember that upheaval
in a few generations or less
can bring us renewal for decades, even longer.
Be positive, keep hoping,
beyond your temporary distress.

Zeal without knowledge is fire without light.
Thomas Fuller

Proposal

Australopithecines roamed the savanna
with brains of only 450cc.
In Homo sapience to 1350cc it grew to be.
Consciousness evolved, increased with size.
Nature called for her understanding, explanations,
and thus the growing mind set out to "fictionalize"
that which man saw with his eyes.
Language was the means to name things and ideas
and to create the coherence of groups,
for nations to arise.
Religions, small and great,
with their rituals arose for this task.
And, paternalistic as they were,
the chief deity was assigned
to maintain adherence to their ethics
not always kind, sometimes malign, but rigidly defined.
But the way we humans are built
there's always a variation of beliefs
towards which one can tilt.
Oh, the fictions we are able to quilt.

Make things as simple as possible,
but not simpler.
Albert Einstein

28

Care Taking

When Spunky and Hidie
took their leave after eighteen years,
I felt the need for a new companion
to greet me coming home,
to need, to sleep, and to talk to me,
in short, to share my affairs.
But at my age of then eighty years
a new kitten would surely outlive me, I feared.
Then I was offered by a friendly soul
to take care of my new companion
for the years after I had outlived my role.
Another party was similarly kind,
alas, both parties eventually changed their minds.
Now I grieve for my beautiful, willful,
Calico-tortoiseshell friend
for what may befall her once I've reached my end.
But who knows, there's always that hope
that she'll find a good home,
for my fears to transcend.

Everything comes to us from others.
To be is to belong to someone.
Jean Paul Sartre

Gibbons

----

also called lesser apes.
Like us other bigger apes,
orang utans, bonobos, gorillas,
humans and chimps,
make do without tails.
I do not see them being in any way "less,"
for when they brachiate through the canopy of trees,
they do this in leaps of up to fifty feet
and at over thirty mph of speed.
I wonder though with how many broken bones,
they must deal?
Yet, it's a marvel to watch them swing
with the agility, the daring, their gracefulness.
And, last not least, to hear them "sing."

You can't do anything about the length of your life,
but you can do something about its width and depth.
Henry Louis Mencken

Science Fiction

I love the subject,
read it for seventy years,
the "hard" kind, that is,
not the fantasy type.
Learned a lot from it,
of history and science,
but skepticism, too,
the generic kind,
also of what was predicted
and what became true.

I've had a lot of worries in my life,
most of which never happened.
Mark Twain

I Love You

What is it that we mean by it?
Is it Eros, sexual love,
or Agape, her spirit?
Is it Intellect expressing itself?
Can it, at times, be all three?
Is it possible to so excel?
Is it just hormones to reach this apogee?
Are mind and body sometimes in harmony?
All too often we aren't conscious, aware,
which of the three has us ensnared.
Does it extend to just human kin,
or will it gather all life,
the Earth, and her oceans in?
What is it when my cat or some creature
seeks physical touch?
Is it recognition of the Self
or is it love?

The greatest achievement of the human spirit
is to live up to one's opportunities and
make the most of one's resources.
Luc de Clapiers de Vauvenargues

Impetus

---

or lack thereof I face.
To overcome the lethargy,
getting the darn derriere into gear.
The prednisone has been ramped down,
but the cortisone won't come around,
and may take months, even a year to rebound.
What will I do with the lack of oomph
for the time ahead,
till my strength may resume?
Ah, the lack of steroids,
what can I say,
stress may cause the adrenal gland
to produce more,
but I need it long-term,
not just for a day.

Life's a tough proposition,
and the first hundred years are the toughest.
Wilson Mizner

Right or Wrong

Good and evil.
How did they arise?
When did they begin?
Consciousness begat us these twins.
Without it animals know no sin.
The growing brain,
evolution so ordained,
enabled the Mind
to determine what was wrong
and what was right,
to help us social animals
to invent nations and religions
to further our kind.
But without beliefs and religions,
their morals and ethics,
there are no wrongs and there are no rights,
there is no good and there is no evil.
Believe me, dear reader:
Nature just is!

Life resembles a novel more often
than novels resemble life.
George Sand

Scylla and Charybdis

The irresistible monsters in the Strait of Messina
Odysseus had to pass.
Also known as:
"Between a rock and a hard place,"
or
"Between the devil and the deep blue sea."
That's where I find myself with my steroid therapy.
The artificial steroid, prednisone, I am to leave be,
I have been on for more than a year,
causing physical and mental upsets and lethargy.
For, my adrenal glands,
once the prednisone was applied,
ramped down their production of cortisol,
nature's natural steroid.
And the body will need months, even a couple of years
to hopefully get back into gear.
With both steroids down I need some stress to come around.
"Given the opportunity, Odysseus,
to face your monsters at Messina,
I'd be happy to volunteer."

There is no cure for birth and death
save to enjoy the interval.
George Santayana

Madagascar Palm

---

properly called Pachypodium lamerei,
is not a palm but rather a succulent.
Mine has a trunk more than four inches thick.
It is twelve feet tall and likely thirty-five years old.
In the course of the years it bloomed threefold.
Like many Madagascar plants it has spines
all over its branches and bole
and its leaves are toxic, I am told.
On the second day in the house,
Rikki, my cat, raced up the tree like a monkey,
halfway up, the force of the impact
toppled the palm and broke some branches.
But not one of her paws was injured
as far as I could see.

You have to decide even to hesitate.
Stanislaw Jerzy Lec

Spammers

Rather useless phones have become
with all these spammers on the run.
No day does pass without five or six,
calls that is, it is a hex.
One can reduce them by Do Not Call,
but it doesn't take long
for them again to sprawl.
A nuisance they are,
making me ignore numbers I don't know.
Yet it may mean that I do miss some
which are important, not containing spam.
What's worse there may be one to strike a chord:
a spam- and tax-free true reward.
If one could only turn the tide
and click to return a destructive broadside.

America is the only country that went from barbarism
to decadence with our civilization in between.
Oscar Wilde

Identity 1

Growing up we are faced with
establishing who we are.
As individuals, first of all,
then to answer a larger call.
For many it's a struggle,
few truly succeed,
and those who fail their lives often cede.
Some find identity in a larger call,
by belonging to a group, a belief,
they fall with in thrall.
Some become terrorists rejecting life,
others may answer to a positive drive.
To find who we are is a never ending road,
for some, at least, most though corrode
and exist without ever becoming,
"becoming," that is, being their ultimate goal.

To fear love is to fear life,
and those who fear life are already three parts dead.
Bertrand Russel

Three grand essentials to happiness in this life
are something to do, something to love,
and something to hope for.
Joseph Addison

To live is the rarest thing in the world.
Most people exist, that is all.
Oscar Wilde

It is not the years in your life
but the life in your years that counts.
Adlai E. Stevenson

Life is a mirror, if you frown at it, it frowns back;
if you smile, it returns the greeting.
William Makepeace Thackeray

Identity 2

I am who I am,
as I've said before.
But there are two "who" meanings,
one claiming the general fact
of my personality, my nature, my persona,
the entire act.
The second "who"
is what makes up these three,
to which I can state
that I know my personality,
with its strengths and weaknesses,
its failures and wins,
its knowledge and ignorance,
and more such twins.
Which returns me again to
I am who I am.

I am the only person in the world
I should like to know thoroughly.
Oscar Wilde

Size Matters

Buntings give way to mourning doves
and lions to elephants do.
Cheetahs find prey among antelopes
and jackals steal from
what the big boys produced.
Among birds the female oft is the bigger one,
and she's the one to set the tone.
Sexual dimorphism, the latter is called.
It also applies to us humans
where the male is usually bigger by twenty percent,
thus tends to garner the rewards,
except when the female has the greater intelligence.
But with humans other matters enter the game,
like education and wealth and status to name.
Just look at the king of the Asian Thai
who deals with his subjects sitting on his dais.
They, groveling – it is hard to behold –
before him as if he were a god.

The gods are on the side of the stronger.
Publius Cornelius Tacitus

To Ika

Mögen die Tage die uns sind verblieben
genügen für unsren Rückblick aufs Leben,
worauf wir hofften und wonach wir strebten.
Wir füllten unser Leben nach bestem Mass,
Du, Ika und Hans,
trocken jedoch ist nun das einst grüne Grass.
Für die Dir verbliebenen Tage –
ich bin knapp hinter her –
wünsch ich Dir Frieden und Liebe
von jenseits dem Meer.

May the days left to us for our life's review suffice
for that which we hoped for and aspired.
As far as we could we filled our lives,
you, Ika and Hans,
dry though now is the once green grass.
For the days left to you
– I am close behind –
I wish you peace and love
from the ocean beyond.

The events we most desire do not happen; or,
if they do, it is neither in the time nor in the circumstances
when they would have given us extreme pleasure.
Jean de la Bruyere

Tinnitus

I've lived with tinnitus for decades.
In the course of time
it was contained and ignored.
In the morning of March 2019
I woke with a persistent high-pitched whine
in my left ear, that is,
where resides my Meniere's disease,
which struck me with its vertigo
nearly two years ago.
Since March this new tinnitus persists on and off.
The audiologist confirmed an additional hearing loss.
And, lo, in my right ear I now have a different ring.
It sounds a bit like music not the whining din.
But – today is the sixty-eighth day
without my having fallen to vertigo's prey.
Maybe there's hope for this affliction to fade?
Come to think of it – I'd rather take the tinnitus
than frequent vertigo events
with their disabling body purges
causing so much dismay.

Some virtues are seen only in affliction
and others only in prosperity.
Joseph Addison

43

One-Armed

I recall a statement of Montaigne's
wherein he suggested we probe the mystery of everyday things.
The below is not an everyday one,
for the loss of a limb is not a minor address.
What this means a recent event drove home.
Breakthrough-bleeding at my right elbow, a rather large splotch,
required the dressing to be changed every day.
While I still have limbs, did not lose an arm,
it is rather awkward to apply, to dress,
with the less dexterous left hand a non-stick patch,
then wind the dressing, the gauze,
around the right elbow, not making a mess.
It made me think of the many women and men
who lost limbs in a mishap or war.
Then, there is Miles O'Brien,
a man I respect, science journalist of PBS,
who lost much of his left arm a few years ago
following an accident in the Philippines.
He usually shows up without a prosthesis on TV.
I have wondered when he will get a functional, mechanical arm,
to, like many others, find ease for his daily activities to perform.

Be kind, for everyone you meet is fighting a hard battle.
Plato

Götz von Berlichingen

There's another story of a one-armed man,
known as the roguish "Knight of the Iron Hand."
I have a slight connection, short of kin.
Just past the Middle Ages in one of his fights,
he lost his right hand,
had an iron-one fashioned alright
with which he continued his armored blight.
Goethe wrote a play
in which the Götz is supposed to have cried
to the delegate having asked for surrender,
the Götz not so inclined:
"Er kann mich im Arsche lecken,"
"He can lick my ass,"
not the sanitized "kiss."
It's now the Swabian Salute,
I take the liberty to boot.
Thus, historically, it's a German invention,
any argument is mute!

As long as war is regarded as wicked
it will always have its fascinations.
When it is looked upon as vulgar, it will cease to be popular.
Oscar Wilde

45

Massage Therapist

A private one, it is, I have.
She leaps on me, then, with her feet,
commences her rhythmic therapy.
If only I were able to
induce her to move her therapeutic massage
to different locations on my fuselage.
Alas, her stomping is instinctive, ingrained.
I wonder what goes on in my Rikki-cat's brain?

All life is an experiment.
The more experiments you make the better.
Ralph Waldo Emerson

Birds

The grosbeaks have arrived for the summer.
A pretty black, brown, orange, and white-colored bird.
They live in families, often five, not quite a herd.
The lazuli buntings are passing through on their way up north.
The males are gorgeously colored
with their blue heads, black,
orange and white-striped bodies.
Except for the raptors, whose females
don't look much different from the males,
the females of smaller birds
feature a more drab coloration than their mates.
It helps to protect them from predation
while they brood their eggs.
Interestingly, human males make do with a paler dress,
while human females are the colorful sex.
Does this imply that they are more secure,
less subject to predation?
Do they live in a safer world
than their smaller avian kin
despite their obvious allure?

As soon as there is life there is danger.
Ralph Waldo Emerson

Empty

---

is the house without my Rikki-cat,
who I had to bring early this morning to the vet
for some tests to make sure she is healthy
as good as it gets.
I do miss the little willful being!
We talk with each other
not always understanding well,
but she tells me when she wants to be fed,
to turn on the faucet at the bathtub
to get her fill.
And when I approach her at her favorite spot,
the bedroom sliding door,
where she watches chipmunks a lot,
she turns over on her back,
offers her white belly for a decent rub.
In the evening she does the same
when I turn off TV.
The silence seems to be a blessing,
and there comes the turnover
for a rub of her belly.

True love is like ghosts,
which everyone talks about and few have seen.
François de La Rochefoucauld

Tourism

---

is degrading the sites
the tourists come to see,
if not physically
then by their sheer quantity.
Increased global wealth
has led to this anomaly,
just as these numbers
are an expression of
our ever increasing
global demography.

What we obtain too cheap, we esteem too little;
it is dearness only that gives everything its value.
Thomas Paine

Wood Fire

Nearby a wood fire burns.
Through my open door
I savor its scent.

There is no reality except the one contained within us.
That is why so many people live such an unreal life.
They take the images outside of them for reality
and never allow the world within to assert itself.
Hermann Hesse

50

Exploration

No, not the exploration of physical sites,
like the cenotes of Yucatan,
the Galapagos, the Himalayas, or the Amazon.
Nor the political questions
of what should and should not be,
since I can't vote anyway.
In the time I have left I want to explore,
to probe, to understand,
maybe create something new.
There are the immaterial questions
of where we come from, why we are as we are,
what drives us, what the world is made of,
the whys, the why nots, the how comes,
what we are failing to see.

Life reflects your own thoughts back to you.
Napoleon Hill

Road Accidents

No road accident has been my fate
for fifty-eight of my years.
I've bashed in a few of my cars
on driveways that is.
I've been an aggressive-defensive driver,
so, was it luck, or my driving ways?
Or, as one of my friends suggested:
"Maybe both."

Do not be too squeamish about your actions.
All life is an experiment.
Ralph Waldo Emerson

Me

The other day I saw my PA
at the hematologist's office
where only five males
but about thirty females are employed, I'd say.
When the PA, Kim, asked me:
"How are you?"
I responded with an emphatic:
"Shitty," that should do.
Right then she dragged me to the offices' other end,
where several tubs of ice cream
where waiting for the employees to attend.
While I was helping myself to a little bit,
I was suddenly surrounded by five svelte females,
in their thirties, I'd bet.
I couldn't help asking:
"Have you come for the ice cream or me?"
Alas, they were honest
in what they had to say.

Youth is a blunder; manhood a struggle;
old age a regret.
Benjamin Disraeli

Goodness Gracious!

Misery it is! I am depressed.
For 74 days I've had no Meniere's attack.
Now, in two days three six-hour events
have laid me back.
And dizziness still accompanies my walk.
My reading has shrunk to almost nil
with my vision impaired,
despite two magnifiers I obtained.
So, what is left to do, but sleep,
that by day, and go to bed by seven or eight?
Watch some TV, here and there write a verse.
And my Rikki's belly was shaved of some fur
for an ultrasound to occur.
I've lost the assurance, or rather she has,
to be taken care upon my demise.
I often think what her life will be like.
The hematologist, Dr. Hamarneh,
has kept me alive to a 200,000 dollar tune.
But what good is it,
if I am not worth much anymore,
just cost money and resources?
Would I not be better off out the door?

Cooked two meals today, will host a friend.
But what is the use without being truly on the mend?
When every two weeks another affliction,
minor or major, raises its ugly head,
calling for another visit to the ER, the GP,
for antibiotics, or what else.
And I'm tired of the discourtesy, the droning on,
of one of our foursome group of "friends."
Then there's the one who left four years ago
for a reason I still don't quite know.
And when you suggest
friend Michel de Montaigne
to write about the mysteries of everyday life,
then let me respond that these days
they are rather mundane,
or worse, they are more likely a pain.
Goodness Gracious,
what a mess the above is.

Life is simply what our feelings do to us.
Honore de Balzac

Factual

Most people take the world for granted,
factual, that is,
and rarely if ever delve into what lurks beneath,
that which is made up,
story tales, unreal.
So much is decreed by language, culture,
which opens itself only to observation,
to awareness to be revealed.
Some even don't know
the difference between opinion
and TRUE fact
to forever travel this shadowland
of mistaken beliefs.

Consistency is the last refuge of the unimaginative.
Oscar Wilde

Confrontation

When in exploring a statement is made
or a question is asked, the respondent's duty,
if he or she is truly engaged,
is to ask further questions like
"Why do you think so?
What does this mean to you?
Where does it come from??"
and more.
In this way the participants can continue
to learn, understand, and explore.
When the partner in conversation responds with
"So what?" or "I disagree,"
the setting is usually ready
for a confrontational spree.
Voices are raised,
a sure sign of disagreement,
and understanding is lost.
For only beliefs back and forth are tossed.
So, don't shoot your mouth off.
Rather let questions be heard.

Even a thought, even a possibility, can shatter us
and transform us.
Friedrich Nietzsche

57

Wordplay

In my teens I read a lot,
what with the dearth of friends I faced.
Thus, when I entered my twenties
a good command of German I had.
And with my social contacts expanding,
punning is what I often did.
I had four years of English at school, after which I was kicked out.
Took evening classes in English on my own,
used it on travels without causing a groan.
But when I came to Canada in '64
I found my English wanting.
Unable to express myself
as I was used to in German, I became insecure,
felt mentally and socially stifled.
As years went by and I once more read a lot,
my English improved, became better than most.
And once more it became fun to pun, whenever a situation offered itself
– and there are many in daily life –
to enjoy playing with words, to elicit a smile or laugh
from those who appreciate not taking life too seriously.

As was his language so was his life.
Lucius Annaeus Seneca

Shadows

Some of us cast shadows
in which others find shade.
Sooner or later
some rather seek sunshine
for which they will trade.
Some will forever accept their fate,
others will escape
to cast their own kind of shade.

Always remember that your decision to be a success
is more important than anything else.
Abraham Lincoln

When It Counts

I pun a lot,
at times, do not speak truth,
exaggerate, do pull a leg,
sometimes push it. What the heck?
Thus I've often told friends,
even people just met, to make amends:
"Don't always trust what I'm saying.
It's often absurd, just for fun,
to nothing does it amount.
But watch out and be aware,
for the times
when it truly counts."

Sway

Out my window I watch
sway in the wind's gentle squalls,
a Sequoia sempervirens
planted there twenty-six years ago,
by now at least forty feet tall.
The swaying's so sensuous,
her branches so lithe,
they remind me of a young woman's movement
so graceful, so charming,
a beautiful aesthetic win.

If your head tells you one thing,
and your heart tells you another,
before you do anything,
you should first decide
whether you have a better head or a better heart.
Marilyn vos Savant

Raccoons

I extend my respect to Procyon lotor
colloquially known as raccoon.
I love the critter's bandit mask,
his dexterous, fingered paws,
his getting into trouble
and endearing chutzpah.
Omnivorous, he eats everything
he can get his "hands" on.
In that, too, he's like us,
Homo sapiens, the not-so-wise-man.
And when he's sometimes destructive
when trying to find food,
he topples the one or other garbage can,
that's just another similarity he has with Man.
So, when the time comes and we are long gone,
I hope the raccoons will rise on their hind legs
and take over from us
for better or worse.

I believe I've found the missing link
between animal and civilized man. It's us.
Konrad Lorenz

Good and Bad

I, at times, like to sneak into a verse
a more or less slanderous remark
about the human race.
At root I know we want to be good,
but all too often we fail to do that which we should
when at heart we know
- or is it again should -
that we really could.
On the other hand,
what's going on today
is causing me no little dismay.

Be able to notice all the confusion
between fact and opinion that appears in the news.
Marilyn vos Savant

Globalization

We have been heading for quite a few years,
actually quite a few thousand it appears,
to ever larger communities.
These days we are connected more than ever before
by air, the media, and electronics galore.
Remember the Thai kids trapped in a cave,
how many across the globe followed their fate,
and the different nationals from across the world
were involved to see them saved?
And let's not forget trade.
Just look at the displays in a grocery store
where we find what was once seasonal produce
any time of the year.
Yes, global trade and technology have also upset
established production and work
having spread loss of self-worth, even fear.
But across the globe it has also delivered
better living conditions to many a peoples' cheer.
Let us hope we find ways to keep globalization going,
for the world has become one without some not yet knowing.

If though wilt make a man happy, add not unto his riches
but take away from his desires.
Epicurus

Banter

I love to banter with (some)
of the many gals
who staff my hematologist's locale.
Having supplied them a few times
with Easter eggs and cookies,
I've made myself a kind of name,
maybe a little kooky, but not bad,
enough for an occasional hug or pat.
So, when I recently had an exchange with three
I said what else is there left to me,
that is, at my age of almost eighty-three,
to corrupt you ladies here and there,
without getting into trouble, as it were?

A man can be happy with any woman,
so long as he does not love her.
Oscar Wilde

Processing

Some people don't listen,
don't hear what's been said,
thus can't process the info
that's been directed to them.
It may leave them confused
or even misled.

Attention-deficit disorders seem to abound in modern society,
and we don't know the cause.
Marilyn vos Savant

Consequences

The all too often results
of earlier desires and decisions
at the time insufficiently examined.
Determined more by wants and emotions,
not seeing or wanting to see
their later repercussions.

Education is learning to grow, learning what to grow toward,
learning what is good and bad,
learning what is desirable and undesirable,
learning what to choose and what not to chose.
Abraham Maslow   0

Bias

We are born to be biased,
whether we want to be or not.
Our thoughts may be weighted in favor or against
a person, a group, a thing, or what else.
Even being aware of a bias we hold,
we still fall victim to its spell.

Be able to recognize when you're reading
or hearing material biased to your own side.
Marilyn vos Savant

Language 1

It's the greatest invention of man,
or might it rather have been developed
by the other more verbal sex, woman?
Fire and tool making, while also important, pale
against the ability of material and immaterial,
spiritual things, to name.
Such as what is a knife and, lo, a wife?
And what is a pigeon versus religion?
The former's substantive, the latter subject to revision.
To create fiction about things that don't even exist.
Different cultures picked different names.
And thus the enormous variety
of different cultures and beliefs became,
spread across the globe,
an encompassing flame.
All too often, though, a mere babble to name.

Habits in writing as in life are only useful if they are broken
as soon as they cease to be advantageous.
William Somerset Maugham

House Cleaning

I have arrived at this stage in my life
when certain things matter more than before.
I think of myself as an avid observer
who values awareness of himself and others, too.
And I want to explore and understand
what the mind and the world are made of
before my time's up, has come to an end.
There are a number of close friends
with whom I can explore,
toss off ideas without offense.
A few others by the wayside went,
one who could not reconcile in his mind,
my comparison of America's president, he supported,
with that of his home country, Turkey,
whose dictator he disliked.
There was another, a good man,
I had hosted for years
who never saw even token reciprocity within his reach,
until I realized he was a leech.

There, too, was a years-long friend
in our discussion group,
who loved confrontation, did not make amends,
and could go on and on to no end.
Confrontation leads nowhere, only voices get loud,
a sign that understanding has been cowed.
There was also a decades-long friend
who, to creationism has been lost.
After I told him about his erroneous belief
our phone calls no longer crossed.
So, here I am, four former friends gone,
but the house now looks cleaner,
no longer rundown.

To be what we are,
and to become what we are capable of becoming,
is the only end of life.
Robert Louis Stevenson

Getting Lost

I never truly got lost in my life,
the physical, not the mental kind.
It was up in Minnesota's lake country wilds
that I took late afternoon a wrong turn
onto a portage I had not in mind.
It was one-hundred degrees, hot as hell,
my sister and her girlfriend, city girls,
and I, pooped as well.
There was bear scat on the portage,
the women freaked out,
we came to its end with another lake in sight.
We stayed there overnight without bears to fight.
I knew where I had gone awry.
Next morning we backtracked,
it was a new day.

In this world there is always danger
for those who are afraid of it.
George Bernard Shaw

Shadowland

Reading an article I came across,
it lamented the Curse of Genius.
Into this category I fall by no means,
I rather think I plopped in between.
Neither fish nor fowl as the saying goes,
I'm neither normal nor highly endowed.
Forever, since I know my IQ,
I have regretted that mine wasn't up the queue.
I just had to make do
with the shadowland's mundane
but acceptable how-to.

A person who doubts himself
is like a man who would enlist in the ranks of his enemies
and bear arms against himself.
He makes his failure certain by himself
being the first person to be convinced of it.
Ambrose Bierce

Reality

Once more, maybe a final time,
I address this vexing subject of what is real,
of objective and fictitious reality,
the two being quite different,
don't correspond, don't chime.
But both are the product of language, of mind.
Objective are a house, a rock, a car.
Fictitious is the concept of nation,
that "all men are created equal,"
and certainly religion.
Most folks do not see
the difference between the two,
and some would strongly disagree
that religion is some comforting ballyhoo.
Yet reality is what it is,
no matter what the shaman says.

We are what we think. All that we are arises with our thoughts.
With our thoughts we make the world.
Buddha

Reverie

Heading straight for my eighty-third year
I keep wondering what all might have happened
to the men and women who once crossed my path,
and wish I had the chance to sit down with them
to chat how they fared over a glass of wine or a beer.
I've never met another one,
who, like myself, was interested to know
how these "old-timers" had done.
Reminisce I do. Does this come with age?
Yet it brings to mind a Shona serpentine sculpture I bought
about twenty years ago at Victoria Falls.
Its creator had named it "Thinking about the Past."
Reverie in English and French
means daydreaming, musing, being lost in thought,
but rêverér means to honor,
and this lies at the root of this pursuit.
I know some of my former friends
have already gone the way of all flesh,
but there must be a few still chipper and fresh.
There comes to mind my buddy of motorcycle fame,
Gernot Winkler, I left behind in Cairo,
who made it to Addis Ababa in time.
Then his track is lost in Africa's dust.

Wilfried Wolf, intrigued by my African exploits,
became a friend, expanding my social horizons.
There was Hannelore Tuberg, precocious as can be.
For some time platonic, ending in a brief erotic spree.
She introduced me to first girlfriend, Ika Illmer, née Obee,
I'm still in touch with, barely, these days.
Her husband Hans just passed away.
There was smart as can be,
Birgitta Forssén on Vänner Lake's shore.
Her brother Carl, aged twelve, on the spur of the moment,
I took to Germany for him to learn more.
Or Herbert Carl who traveled with me up to Sweden
trying to capture this attractive Birgitta maiden.
And not to forget a most important friend,
Horst Nitschke by name, who, from East Germany had come.
Just made it in time to get out, as it were,
he had been an FDJ Funktionär.
Another world, he too, opened up,
but the last time I tracked him down years past
to ascertain he was alive,
I must assume that by now he's left this life.
Milton Surajit Kumar Guha Thakurta,
an Indian born in the city of Calcutta,
from whom I learned that other thought matters.
And Tony Soon Ho from Singapore
I met in Paris at the Alliance Française,

another important friend at the time
who opened to me another world.
There, too, was Otto Schupp, from Switzerland,
he, Soon, and I the Paris dance floors hit.
He later visited me in Chicago,
I in Zürich, where he had married, with two sons to attend.
Then he suddenly was gone.
My Paris co-workers, Michel Mauduit, Marcel Petuaud,
and "grand père" Lemarié who,
with his two daughters, introduced me
to the delights of French cuisine.
Warner and Audrey Clark, Canadian friends,
who, like so many others, left no mark on the Internet,
disappeared having nothing penned.
The above are all people of my distant past.
There are quite a few others
who did not leave their mark
and thus their names to last.
Then there are at least half a dozen friends
of more recent times,
who have traveled this trail of joy and sorrow,
relieved of all travails and concerns of the morrow.
And more will yet go.
Will I eventually be the only one who keeps wondering
what all they experienced, what all they have done?
As a final thought I can't help wondering

what happened to the hippos, the elephants, the giraffes,
the wildebeest, the baboons, the impala, and zebras,
the wart hogs, the buffalo, the lions and cheetahs,
the many other creatures whose paths I crossed
in Africa's savannas, waters, bush and forest.
And except for the long-lived elephants
most are likely already gone.

One can be master of what one does,
but never of what one feels.
Gustave Flaubert

Contacts

For fifteen months now I conscientiously am
going weekly to Dr. Hamarneh's Prescott Valley "harem,"
there to have my blood tested and being infused
for my hemolytic anemia to remain defused.
The office employs only five men
but close to thirty women.
I know quite a few after all this time,
like Joline, Kelli, Adrienne, her daughter Iris,
Kimberly, Jessica, Heather, and, not to forget Jennifer,
who, the other day, somewhere hearing my voice
found me for a hug, her choice.
Maybe my cookies and Easter eggs did their thing,
but it must be some more:
my banter, my respect and wit.
Do I hear vanity ring?

Behind many acts that are thought ridiculous
there lie wise and weighty motives.
François de La Rochefoucauld

Heretic

What a proud designation to be.
Not a yes-sayer, a believer, a follower,
but someone independent and free.
Except when his belief is just a modification
of what he doesn't agree.

Rather fail with honor than succeed by fraud.
Sophocles

Chicken Tikka Masala

---

was once only roasted marinated "tikka," meat.
But the Brits preferred it saucy,
which is why an Indian or Pakistani
created the sauce of yoghurt, spices and cream.
Which, together with fish and lamb,
for an aficionado, tastes like a dream.

Nothing is more difficult, and therefore more precious,
than to be able to decide.
Napoleon I

Lion Fish

It must have been in seventy-two
when I snorkeled in Moorea's lagoon.
Between the snorkel and the flippers
I did not wear a costume.
Approaching the shallows,
observing the sea life left and right,
I suddenly had a lion fish in my sight,
or rather it was him or her
which stared at me in my plight.
In shallow water of just a couple of feet
have you ever tried paddling backwards with flippers
to get away as fast as possible
before one of its stingers might smite?

All life is an experiment.
The more experiments you make the better.
Ralph Waldo Emerson

Sister's Keeper

The other day I had lunch with a friend.
I ordered a cup of soup, a Reuben, and some Chardonnay.
The service was slow, my friend commented so.
I did not mind since we had plenty to say.
When my check arrived the soup was amiss.
On the spur of the moment I asked my vis-a-vis:
"Brothers Keepers,"
do you think we should be?
It took him a moment to agree.
Following this adage should I then tell the waitress
about her having missed the soup of the day?
Thus I politely pointed it out to the miss,
which she took in stride while I paid for the forgotten dish.
I couldn't help feeling honest but also stupid
by having supported the inattentive lass,
or rather the restaurant to my disadvantage.

If you can do a half-assed job of anything,
you are a one-eyed man in the kingdom of the blind.
Kurt Vonnegut

Beholden

Ah, the reaction of those who whatever behold
to respond defensively to what they are told.
Instead of weighing the matter's truth,
they quite often come up with an excuse.
Truth isn't helped by such abuse.
Comprehension and learning are pushed aside.
It's much easier to keep beholding
for an easier ride.

I live in terror of not being misunderstood.
Oscar Wilde

Pontificating

By gosh, I've been accused of this,
to speak pompously and dogmatically,
I must watch my talk, not become remiss.
But then it occurred to me about the other's stance:
Where did he pick up this word?
Was where he came from just ignorance?

Do not impose on others what you yourself do not desire.
Confucius

Gift

For a year-and-a-half it's been my weekly task
to drive to my hematologist's office
to have drawn some blood into a little flask
and to consult with the doc what's next to ask.
By now I know and am known
with my bantering style, by a number of women
of which there are close to thirty, I'm told,
versus only five males in the entire hold.
When recently I registered,
exchanged some words with the receptionist,
to then sit down in the waiting room,
one of my favorite gals,
her office down the aisle,
suddenly stood before me and remarked:
"I heard your voice
and have come to give you a hug."
A precious gift it was.

Tell me who admires and loves you,
and I will tell you who you are.
Antoine de Saint-Exupery

Dross

In the course of life I have come across
plenty of events, people, and such,
which, when I look back,
were just that much dross.
Which is why I have found, again and again,
greater understanding
in the inquisitive exchange of thoughts,
face-to-face, with a woman or man.
This, versus the yaw yaw of groups,
the backs and forth between everyone,
usually turning out to be dross.
Small loss.

Art is not a handicraft, it is the transmission of feeling
the artist has experienced.
Lev Nicolaevich Tolstoy

Proactive

---

means not to wait for things to happen.
To think ahead, anticipate, prepare.
What are the options? What can be done?
To take control of a situation,
to provide what others leave undone?
Be enterprising, energetic, driven,
and not react only after
something's come along.

Take care to get what you like
or you will be forced to like what you get.
George Bernard Shaw

Oradour-sur-Glane

Seventy-five years ago
German SS-troups massacred,
burned and machine-gunned,
six hundred forty-two inhabitants of the town.
Oh, I weep for you long-gone French citizens!
But what are you
against the more than seventy million dead
this war has cost?!
A miniscule 0.0001 per cent.
I have traveled back in time,
I see the burning, smell the stench,
hear the ratatat of machine guns,
the helpless shouts, the screams, the wails,
then the silence of death once the atrocity ends.
Oh, do I weep for you long-gone
residents of Oradour-sur-Glane.

The only thing that stops God from sending another flood
is that the first one was useless.
Nicolas de Chamfort

Willful

---

stubborn, determined, headstrong,
contrary, recalcitrant, intractable,
wayward, insubordinate, curious,
sometimes cuddly, peaceful,
sociable, talkative, demanding,
volitional, nippy, escape artist,
doing what she wants:
that's my Rikki Tikki Tavi Cat,
and I love her for that,
creature in her own right.

It is easier to suppress the first desire
than to satisfy all that follow it.
Benjamin Franklin

Vaccinations

Once, when there was still trust in the sciences
vaccinations were a matter of course.
And in their daily lives people experienced
the many illnesses manifold curse.
They also were less educated to question
vaccinations' worth.
Today, trust in the sciences has waned
and the many illnesses of the past
have faded,
faded also from the people's minds.
Then, too, there's a semi-educated kind
of mind who believes to know better
what to do and what to mind.
Thus, ignorance, stupidity, and know-it-all
have combined
to make societies fallible
and many people blind.

The mind becomes that which it contemplates.
Percy Bysshe Shelley

Charles Darwin,

liberator of mankind,
who freed the Western World
and all those inclined,
from the biblical errors,
superstitions and falsehoods
of a bygone time.
Yet there are still the many
who believe in a not-so-caring God,
instead of Nature which is as it is,
without reason and mind,
an oh-so-scary perspective,
although this is what the universe is truly like.

Life is beauty, admire it.
Life is a dream, realize it.
Life is a challenge, meet it.
Life is a duty, complete it.
Life is a game, play it.
Life is an opportunity, benefit from it.
Life is a promise, fulfill it.
Life is sorrow, overcome it.
Life is a song, sing it.
Life is a struggle, accept it.
Life is a tragedy, confront it.
Life is an adventure, dare it.
Life is luck, make it.
Life is life - fight for it.
Unknown

Paranoia

A mental condition prone
to delusions of persecution,
unjustified jealousy,
exaggerated self-importance,
even schizophrenia,
where the person loses touch with reality.
There too is obsession, megalomania,
monomania, even psychosis,
and mistrust of people without evidence.
Now, imagine a country
governed by such excellence.

The first method for estimating the intelligence of a ruler
is to look at the men he has around him.
Nicolo Machiavelli

Defensiveness

Ah, the rare woman or man
who need not respond
to criticism, a challenge.
Who securely rests in the knowledge
of who he or she is,
and, to what others may say,
doesn't give a damn.

Only the shallow know themselves.
Oscar Wilde

Weapons

I have collected a number of weapons,
Sumatran swords, daggers, and such.
There's a Maori patu,
a Hawaiian pololu shark tooth sword
and Polynesian mace, a bludgeon,
a seventeenth century dueling pistol,
an African authority staff,
its knob also serving nicely as a club.
Yet, there's also an aboriginal collecting basket
and a calabash, plus a Haida drum.
All mementos of an anthropologist,
at heart a peaceful man.

Every creature lives in a state of war by nature.
Jonathan Swift

Being

There is this rock I squat upon.
Rikki, from her cave, observes.
as do I,
watching branches and twigs swerve
sensuously in the occasional breeze.
Movements they repeat
in an everlasting entreat.
A breath of wind flutters by my ears.
A lizard pumps on a boulder.
The occasional bird flits by
daring to come near.
I know all this will come to an end.
The winds will die down.
Precious silence will reign.
And I?
I just am.

Never express yourself more clearly than you think.
Niels Bohr

Shadow

These days,
at times,
I sense it approaching
from behind,
a shadowy figure,
gently touching my body, my mind.
It does not speak,
does not have need.
It knows I understand,
but the time isn't yet ripe.
But soon, it nears,
there is this call
to leave this valley of tears.
But until then
there's still some pleasure, some joy,
if only to hug my not-so-named
Helen of Troy.

You can't have everything.
Where would you put it?
Steven Wright

Relationships

It's been a puzzle why some folks brag:
"Oh, I have that many grandchildren."
What the heck!
Traveling in time many years back,
my wife and I were invited as honor guests
to a friend's family gathering of more than one hundred
from one family side only, quite a pack.
An improbable attempt
to collect family members from both sides of mine
would most likely be limited by some thirty-nine.
There are three grandkids, two girls and a boy.
The girls' surnames are different, of course,
the boy was not given my family name.
Who am I to blame?
There is one other family branch with two girls only,
causing the family name to be stanched.
Sometimes I regret for it to disappear.
It's a good name to see, to hear.
But then I think: What's in a name?
What counts is that life goes on.
And think: A grandchild carries only
twenty-five per cent of one's genes,
from where it diminished to twelve, then six,

all becoming washed out in time by the forthcoming mix.
So I comfort myself that life must go on.
A name doesn't really matter that much
if there's always a new dawn.

You can't depend on your eyes
when your imagination is out of focus.
Mark Twain

Language 2

- -

Without language,
what would we be?
Just another animal
with a max of thirty sounds
to warn and to flee.

The trouble with the world is that the stupid are cocksure
and the intelligent are full of doubt.
Bertrand Russell

Beer

I drink little alcohol,
just some here and there.
A bottle of beer, for instance,
is often more for all I care.
Now, I've found cerveza Coronita,
just right for me.
If you don't speak Spanish
and know nothing of cereveza, beer:
It's means little Corona, crown, my dear.

The simplest questions
are the hardest to answer.
Northrop Frye

Axis of Rotation

In its orbit around the sun,
the 23.5 degree tilted Earth's axis of rotation
is fixed with respect to the star,
thus points toward or away from the sun.
This causes the seasons alternating
between the northern and southern hemisphere.
Could I have only experienced the Alaskan
all day sunshine, 80 days at Barrow,
all day night for 67 days.
Brrrr, both ways.

Some would like to understand what they believe in.
Others would like to believe what they understand.
Stanislaw Jerzy Lec

Effort of Will

With my prednisone low
and the cortisol too,
there's not enough steroid
to make me go.
Lethargy rules
and it takes a decision,
an effort of will,
to get going on something
instead of falling asleep.
When, if ever, will I be humming again?

The trouble with our times is
that the future is not what it used to be.
Paul Valery

Mysterious

---

is the world we inhabit,
the lives we live.
This is how a friend increasingly
sees the world.
Nothing wrong with it,
for it is correct.
All too often it is puzzling, strange,
bizarre, inexplicable, bewildering,
unfathomable, and obscure.
Yet there's this other approach
called science,
trying to unravel these mysteries.
It attempts to explain, to fathom,
decipher, decode, to penetrate,
and to reveal the secrecies
this world of ours holds.
Both stances have their value,
but while I marvel at the mysteries,
there's this challenge to unravel
them, so manifold.

We live by information, not by sight.
Balthasar Gracian

Caveat

When it comes to praise there's a difference between
Americans and Germans,
although that's not the only one to name.
Americans are more accepting,
one aspect of their culture, "e pluribus unum,"
"Out of many, one,"
was, until recently, the way it was done.
An American can praise, simply to praise,
or overlook a deficiency, hoping the future will,
whatever the issue, the subject upraise.
When a young German goes to his task master
to show what he has done, the master might say:
"You did fine, my son,"
followed by:
"But if you would move this little screw
two centimeters to the left,
your result would even be better, I'm certain of that."
All too often there's this caveat, beware,
rarely is a German praise without impair.

One can always be kind to people
about whom one cares nothing.
Oscar Wilde

Compulsion

By gosh, today, a psychologist
called me a compulsionist.
Allow me here to play once more
with the American language I adore.
As if I were forced to do what I don't care for.
It is claimed that there is a constraint
which keeps me in thrall,
a force, a pressure, an obligation,
an irresistible urge to act
against my conscious wishes,
but that's not even all.
I do what I like and that is it.
Whether it is compulsive or not,
I give a scat.
But in the final consequence I must admit,
my "psycho" friend isn't out of his wit.

Too much work and too much energy kill a man
just as effectively as too much assorted vice or too much drink.
Rudyard Kipling

Sundowner

Coming to the end of a game drive
we stop in a clearing,
maybe on a knoll,
in African safari country,
the sun nearing its goal.
The surroundings are clear,
the setting picturesque,
but this is lion country,
caution is a must.
We get off the truck,
gather at its rear.
The gate comes down
for a mini-bar to appear.
We collect our drinks,
and socialize in the wilds,
there is no better setting,
hardly better times.

When the time comes in which one could,
the time has passed in which one can.
Marie von Ebner-Eschenbach

Timid

Some of us grow up this way,
others are given it by their DNA.
The timid ones are protected
from getting into much trouble.
They drift though life,
let others have their say.
For the bolder ones
life, at times, is more of a struggle.
While they succeed in many things,
they also fail, do not always win.
And there are times when fate clips their wings.
But on the whole, being bold serves them well.
Lucky, if they don't believe
that there ain't no heaven
and there ain't no hell.

Success is dependent on effort.
Sophocles

Adherents

We live by the myths created by man,
and women, too, I am sure.
Without them societies could neither exist
or quickly fall apart.
But don't tell people they believe in myths
which, for many, are dear to their hearts.
However, for those who doubt,
thinking our rules are just a scam,
in the back of their minds
they adhere to them anyway,
for they sense that if people
no longer believe in them,
it's the end of the whole shebang.

When you have eliminated the impossible,
whatever remains, however improbable, must be the truth.
Arthur Conan Doyle

Change

There was this boy in his early teens,
like many a kid
was going to change the world,
dump much of what he had picked up
or what he had otherwise learned.
Some considered him a living corpse,
but inside it roiled and boiled.
The restlessness took him abroad,
and in due course he learned a lot.
What was procured in the restless mind
eventually came to the fore.
Some was for the better,
some caused no little uproar.
But in the end it did produce
an independent mind,
broadly based, an unconventional kind.

The average value of conversation could be enormously improved
by the constant use of four simple words:
"I do not know."
André Maurois

Cathedrals

I admire the European cathedrals
but some of them are too ornate.
I'd rather wander sequoia forests
where giants to the heavens reach.

Nothing is great or little otherwise
than by comparison.
Jonathan Swift

Credulous

There are people who are disposed
to take anecdotal events
far too easily, uncritically, as fact.
And, impressionably,
with more such anecdotal events,
create their unique personal world,
fictitious at best.
They want to believe,
when they ought to be doubtful,
questioning, dubious, too,
and give anecdotal events their skeptical due,
for a more incredulous world view.

I do not believe in the collective wisdom
of individual ignorance.
Thomas Carlyle

The Promise

When I promise my Rikki
I'll take her out for a walk,
in the coming morning or eve,
this promise, of course, is not to my cat,
but is rather to keep it myself,
and that's a fact.

Responsibility is the price of freedom.
Elbert Hubbard

Promises

And is it not that the promises we make
are not for the receiver,
including the self,
but always for ourselves to keep?

Necessity is no law.
Benjamin Franklin

Promising

All too often a promise is made:
"I'll bring you such-and-such
next time we meet."
Or another assurance
which isn't maintained,
like "I'll be in touch," but never am.
Is it that people's memory fails
or that, already when mouthed,
they never intend to pay up
to what they claim?

Our memories are independent of our wills.
Richard Brinsley Sheridan

Monsoon

The land is thirsty,
the ground is parched.
The DG, decomposed granite, where I live,
to call soil would be too much to ask.
This winter's rainfalls and a couple of snows,
seeped slowly into the ground
for trees and bushes to still grow.
But the small plants and grasses
are withered and glum.
The middle of July it is.
Monsoon, monsoon, you are needed,
do come.
Some nice thunderstorms
to replace the blue skies,
would be most welcome.

We do not succeed in changing things according to our desire,
but gradually our desire changes.
Marcel Proust

Senescence

Two long-time friends,
one close, the other an ocean apart,
both about my age,
their minds no longer doing their part.
One is aware of his failing mind,
the other denies it
although he is in a more serious bind.
The one overseas I can only worry about,
call him weekly until he disappears to an infirmary
to drop out.
The other, a bright brain,
is aware of his failing mind,
so he isn't going into this shadowland blind.
It is scary to watch once great minds fade away
and be grateful that mine is still functioning,
has not yet gone astray.

Our greatest fears lie in anticipation.
Honore de Balzac

Waiting Room Game

The other day, lo and behold,
a doctor's waiting room kept me on hold.
Busy like I'd rarely seen it before there was a constant back and fro.
of patients coming for dialysis or the doc somehow.
To entertain myself
I neither read, texted, nor played games on my phone.
I began a study of humanity in the room.
Too many had a problem with weight.
How many had taken care of their fate?
There were the ones doing financially well,
from the clothes they wore I could easily tell.
The educational level of others sitting there,
I gave a stab, and wildly guessed if
conservatives or progressives they were.
There were the wives who took care of their husbands,
whether they needed it or not,
which told me if the men were sons of bitches,
easy to judge by their reactions.
At last I was relieved from my wait, called from my observational spate
I told the doc what a motley bunch of patients she had
but wondered where my estimates had failed.

Our future is based on our past.
Paul Valery

Deception

----

is the unkind attempt
to make others believe something untrue
or to gain advantage for oneself.
The worst, though, is the well-known fact
most people readily enact
to deceive themselves,
an anti-intellectual pact.
There is not enough space here
to mention every one,
readily known as self-deception.
A Frenchman, five hundred years ago,
François de La Rochefoucault,
trained his wit on life's varied lore,
the human tendency to deceive oneself,
held tightly by emotional retention
and lack of awareness,
an intellectual whore.

The only thing one can do with good advice
is to pass it on. It is never of any use to oneself.
Oscar Wilde

Profiles

My Rikki-cat's profile is very close
to that of a human's,
except for the frontal lobes.
I wish it were thus
for an even better understanding
between us.

Beyond each corner new directions lie in wait.
Stanislaw Jerzy Lec

Mnemonics

As my short-term memory
at times lets me down,
I develop mnemonic aids
none, though, would earn a triple crown.
"Cortisol" is one that slips,
thus I came up with
"court" and "sol,"
or for the "Dillard" store,
it's "dill," my favorite herb.
For "anecdotal" "doting," is of help,
and "hemoglobin" is accessed
by "globe," with "hemo," blood,
not being a difficult word.
And things to be done
a slip of paper are noted on.
Thus, the "coming of age" of eighty-three
I navigate.
All in all, it isn't yet too bad.

The way to love anything is to realize
that it might be lost.
Gilbert Keith Chesterton

Rain

Finally the rains have come.
Like tears, drops down window panes run.
It is a joy to see them slither,
At last the monsoon blows joyously hither.
An occasional thunderbolt enlivens the sky,
its following thunder the clouds outcry.

The cure for boredom is curiosity.
There is no cure for curiosity.
Dorothy Parker

Black Hole

In the constellation Cygnus, The Swan,
high in the sky,
there lurks a Black Hole
fifteen times the mass of the sun.
Its distance is six thousand light years and some.
It is just a baby as Black Holes come.
From a big companion star nearby
it sucks gases little by little away.
And there dwells a monster Black Hole
in the direction of Sagittarius,
at the center of the Milky Way,
where it gobbles up anything coming near.
But sleep easy my friend,
that's where it will stay.
When you look at the night sky,
so peaceful it seems,
but believe me,
the universe is a violent place.

There are moments when everything goes well,
but don't be frightened, it won't last.
Jules Renard

Intelligent Life

Rarely a day passes when we don't read or hear,
that we might find microbial life in our solar system, here and there,
on Enceladus, on Europa, Titan, or Mars.
Much is unscientific babble,
pie in the sky or dreaming about stars.
But to the stars we need look, among the millions far,
to find, maybe, life similar to ours, or, more likely, bizarre.
While the universe holds all the stuff for life,
it's a giant leap for dead matter to come alive.
From there to intelligence is just as great,
the variables for it to come to be
are too numerous to list here.
They are so plentiful, in fact
that the probability is greatly stacked
to be zero for star peers to contact.
Evolution has no purpose, drive.
It is not out to create intelligent life.
We may be in the Milky Way the only lot
with a modicum of intelligence, whether we like it or not.
And were this our fate, our various religions would celebrate.

Call sense to a fool and he calls you foolish.
Euripides

Belief 1

Half a lifetime ago, my friend Paul
invited me to breakfast
with Edgar Mitchell, Apollo 14 astronaut.
After his 1971 moonwalk and retirement from NASA,
he investigated extrasensory phenomena.
An Asian healer in Houston piqued his interest.
Edgar had his severely vision-impaired mother
driven five hundred miles to Houston.
There, the healer asked the woman to sit on a chair,
close her eyes and keep them closed.
Some time later he asked her to open them.
She did and cried: "I can see. I can see!"
Subsequently she drove herself
the five hundred miles home.
A few days later she called Edgar asking:
"Is this healer a Christian?"
Edgar told his devoutly Christian mother
that the man was not a Christian.
Hearing this, his mother's vision impairment returned.

Nature never deceives us;
it is we who deceive ourselves.
Jean-Jaques Rousseau

Class

It took me a lifetime to learn a few things,
and, still, I mess up here and there.
They aren't major any more
but I cringe the instant I'm aware.
And as is my character I banter a lot,
which can get me close,
well, to my mouth getting shot off.
But there are folks who are ignorant
of what they do or say,
something which left their orifice,
what's called a faux pas.
We are all prone to make social mistakes,
but it is a pleasure to meet someone
who has class
and in all situations knows what to say
or what need not be done.

To succeed in the world it is not enough to be stupid,
you must also be well mannered.
Voltaire

Always

Alone I am,
and yet, I am not.
I yearn for your company
to ease my lot.
I will always love you,
if only for the many years
we've know each other,
for the shared memories
we can recall.
And that is not all.

The only real progress lies in learning
to be wrong all alone.
Albert Camus

Unity

The further we go back in time
the smaller human societies become.
These groups were small,
and they differentiated between "us" and "them."
In time they grew larger,
were united by religions and trade.
And ever so slowly
the "us" and "them" lessened, was caused to fade.
Today, great blocks of nations exist.
The globe is united by science.
And if we aren't messing up,
Earth will eventually be united
in one great cusp.

Blessed is he who expects nothing,
for he shall never be disappointed.
Jonathan Swift

Cetaceans

Not a week passes these days
that we hear or see on TV,
a pod of whales, small and large,
stranded on some beach.
Did this happen as much in previous times,
or is it somehow our doing, our crime?
If it took place in times of old,
fewer people lived and roamed the shores.
And if they came across a stranded pod of whales,
well, these were just animals,
at most a source of oil or meals.
Only today, when people throng beaches
and means and ethics have improved,
will humans engage in rescuing these creatures.
Maybe there's hope for us after all?

The actions of men are the best interpreters
of their thoughts.
John Locke

Nasi Goreng

is Fried Rice in bahasa Indonesia,
the Indonesian language,
rice being the staple
for breakfast, lunch and dinner.
I have eaten it a few times on Sumatra,
consisting of a heap of rice,
a few leaves of vegetable, some sauce,
and a small piece of meat or fish topping it off.
At home I have prepared it many times the Western way,
with five kinds of vegetables,
roasted pork and popcorn shrimp mixed in, spicy and tasty.
Just had a dinner party of nine
treating them to nasi goreng,
topped with roasted peanuts and coconut flakes,
krupuk: tapioca crackers and emping.
Fried bananas, mango chutney, sweet ginger,
cool cucumber slices,
a palliative for heat-sensitive palates,
and deep-fried anchovies.
Barely a rice grain was left on their plates.

After dinner rest a while; after supper walk a mile.
T. Cogan

Scent

My little companion, Rikki-Cat,
by night and by day prefers to sleep
on the chair I sit on at my desk
and for the night put my clothes on.
I wonder whether it is the comfort she derives,
since I prepare her chair for the night,
or might it be
that she's endeared by my scent,
or ought I call it odor with your assent?

Nature has no principles.
She makes no distinction between good and evil.
Anatole France

131

Papaya

It was on one of the Society Islands
that a local showed us his papaya grove,
the papaya being the largest herb known.
He told us that papaya trees
come as females and males,
in saplings not easily shown.
As is common in nature,
one male is enough to fertilize many females,
and the superfluous males are cut down.
Thus, we get this delicious fruit
only from female plants grown.
Is papaya then a euphemism?
Another example of male chauvinism!
Papaya, like Lady Godiva, "Gift of God,"
unfortunately doesn't travel well,
or it would get my daily nod.
And, lo,
mamaya, it therefore ought to be called.

A good idea will keep you awake during the morning,
but a great idea will keep you awake during the night.
Marilyn vos Savant

Bacon 'n Eggs

Sometimes, rarely, I order for myself
a helping of bacon 'n eggs.
Following American custom the eggs
come either "over easy" or "sunny side up."
I like my eggs fried well,
which, besides preferring them this way,
leads to my little setup.
Always up to banter I put the server to a test.
One took me as a foreigner, others smile.
Some are dull, some produce a frown,
when I order my eggs
"sunny side down."

An idea that is not dangerous
is unworthy to be called an idea at all.
Oscar Wilde

Lost

Sometimes, only when it's lost,
does one realize its cost.

Do not walk on a well-trodden path –
you may slip.
Stanislaw Jerzy Lec

God's Creatures

There once was a neighbor
who did not like
the doves gobbling up the bird food
she'd provide.
What comes to my mind
is what mother, in German, would've said:
"They are all God's creatures,"
and that's what she meant.
To this day I still recall her advice.
To my mother they were God's creatures.
To me it describes
the unity of life.

One half, the finest half, of life is hidden from the man
who does not love with passion.
Stendhal

Death Wish

I think I'm honest and don't exaggerate
to consider myself a disciplined man.
Then why is it that I don't do the exercises,
I know will keep me fit,
and if not like Tarzan, a little bit.
There dwells in my mind's kettle of fish
the thought that I'm entertaining
what's called a death wish.

Minds, like bodies, will often fall into a pimpled,
ill-conditioned state from mere excess of comfort.
Charles Dickens

Belief 2

Believe me,
when I say this isn't a pun:
"All beliefs from man's fertile mind have sprung."
Pantheism comes close to mine
without "theos," God,
"pan" being of an all-encompassing sort.
And I'm aware of what I've composed,
according to which I myself comport.
But what of the many who blindly believe
in whatever they've been taught,
rightly or wrongly,
by the human mind conceived?

The worst sin towards our fellow creatures
is not to hate them, but to be indifferent to them;
that's the essence of inhumanity.
George Bernard Shaw

Paper Weights

To protect some of my paper stuff
from being blown off my desk
by wind's capricious momentary gusts,
what serves me as a paperweight
is a little chunk of hematite
I found out in the desert.
A small lump of copper
inherited from my dad,
is one way I remember him.
I saw him handling it,
when I was still a lad.

Commonplace

My friend Montaigne still comes to mind
whenever of commonplace things I write.
He encouraged people to do just that,
to tell about the little events
which life throws at us.

Thinking is the hardest work there is,
which is probably the reason why so few engage in it.
Henry Ford

Aberration 1

To change from a normal mode of conduct
to an abnormal one.
As we ramble on through life,
some of us keep rambling, others keep bumbling,
while some of us are exposed
to an influence different from a "normal" one.
The different ones usually creep up on us.
Eventually, the new mode normal becomes.
Worst are the ones which grow
with power gained or, rarely, bestowed.
Examples are Saddam Hussein,
Gaddafi, Jeffrey Epstein, and Mao.
The old "normal" is forgotten
with the new running wild.
There's rarely a way back.
An adult cannot return to being a child.
Blessed are those who do not fall victim to temptation,
and those who find their way back to
their previous, normal situation.

There are several good precautions against temptation,
but the surest is cowardice.
Mark Twain

Mathematics

One of my great regrets
is my deficiency in understanding mathematics.
These days it is complemented by another branch,
that of statistics.
Alas, I've muddled through life without the two.
And at my age this will have to do.

Two things control men's nature,
instinct and experience.
Blaise Pascal

Ignoramus

When I think of all there is to be known,
yet to explore, to learn,
of people, the mind, and the world,
of things yet unheard,
I must admit, and I'm not at all ashamed,
of what an ignoramus I am.
At least I'm aware while many are not,
which, permit me to say,
leaves much food for thought.
What pleasure it is to here and there
come across what I call:

cognoscente.

No persons are more frequently wrong,
than those who will not admit they are wrong.
François de La Rochefoucauld

Topsy Turvy

The Donald and Boris represent
a topsy turvy world.
For many decades we, kind of, cruised along
safe and sound.
Now the world is turned upside down.
We humans seem to need this once in a while
to stir things up, make a mess of the pile,
only to, hopefully, rise once more
for a better world, another temporary encore.

God created man
because he was so disappointed in the monkey.
Mark Twain

143

Wanted

To be wanted,
shy of love,
would be plenty,
be enough.

Love is like quicksilver in the hand.
Leave the fingers open and it stays.
Clutch it, and it darts away.
Dorothy Parker

Kinship

It is a joy to suddenly find
a flexible, vivacious, intelligent mind,
more than the run-of-the-mill kind.
Nothing is wrong with ordinary folk,
my appreciation is for everyone
who to decency is inclined.
But once in a while there rings a bell,
and knowing one has found
a mind ticking lively in parallel.
What a joy it is to explore a rich mind,
and to know of this kinship
of humankind.

The secrets of life are not shown
except to sympathy and likeness.
Ralph Waldo Emerson

Admission to Ignorance

There is no fault in admitting
to not knowing.
Just the opposite,
it takes self-assurance and strength.
And at its root lies curiosity,
to learn something new,
not to rest on one's laurels,
but go the extra length
to find what's hidden behind the horizon
of human ignorance.
Which is what the sciences did
barely three hundred years ago,
freeing us from the many "stories"
created by man,
the many false "think-we-know."

Our worries come from our weaknesses.
Joseph Joubert

Myopic

People steeped in faith
are incapable of looking left or right.
Among them are good minds,
but wasted they are,
when belief makes them blind.
Amazing is how they can blend out
much of which is rational thought.
You may sit in an airplane
and talk to the person next to you.
She may seem like a normal human being,
but were you to delve a bit deeper,
to find out where she stands,
you'd be shocked and surprised
that she inhabits a crazy no-man's-land.

Anything one man can imagine,
other men can make real.
Jules Verne

147

What Makes You Tick?

You meet someone new
and right away, deep down, you wonder:
What makes your vis-à-vis tick?
What are his motivations?
What is her depth?
What is their education?
Not what they learned in school,
but what they've learned in exploration
of life's vicissitudes,
and how they've dealt with their frustrations.
Alas, few people are prepared to open up,
to relate the private things they do hold back.
It takes a person, unafraid and strong
to exchange their inner being's song.
But when it happens, rarely so,
the world assumes a happy glow.
Oh, what a fool am I to dream as such,
where is the depth to reveal that much?

There is little that can withstand a man
who can conquer himself.
Louis XIV

148

Motive

I am angry, very much so,
to write the below:
The first thing one hears after a killing spree
is to question what the killer's motive might be.
As if this were the cause at root.
People, how stupid can you be!?
Crazy people are there by the dozen,
their motive is craziness in all its variations.
But what is common to every single one
is the easy access to killing guns.
When will the primary question be asked,
and effective gun control be introduced?
And did it ever to the gun-toters occur,
who prevent effective gun control,
that they too are implicated,
responsible, for every murder spree,
every single human being killed this way?
Shame, shame, shame on you
who cannot see,
being beholden by ideology!

A gentleman is one who never hurt's anyone's feelings
unintentionally.
Oscar Wilde

Wit

Can I, should I, should I not
attribute wittiness to me,
it being defined by the below phraseology,
such as mental sharpness, inventiveness,
perception, insight, savvy, sagacity, acuity,
and whatnot?
These days I frequently declaim
that the only part of me that's still aworking
is my brain.
I'm pleased, were it not that the rest of me
is definitely on the wane.

Wit lies in recognizing the resemblance among things
which differ and the difference between things which are alike.
Madame de Stael

To Be Cavalier

It's been said that I'm sometimes cavalier.
No, not King Charles' I, cavalier of old,
but the uncouth character of a different mold,
who's offhand, insouciant, condescending,
disdainful, contemptuous, insolent, and glib,
a couldn't-care-less.
Where I stand these days
I truly do care less.
Yet, deep down,
there are situations, issues, people, and such,
for which I do care very much,
which I revere, respect, admire,
treasure, value, cherish, and love.

What prevents our abandoning ourselves
to a single vice is our having more than one.
François de La Rochefoucauld

I Grieve

A long time ago, almost fifty years,
we became neighbors with this family, friends.
We traveled together. They were caring dears
and made amends for my affairs.
After her mother died religion called.
He became the congregation's organizational man.
After we moved he and I kept in touch by phone.
But more and more his talk,
his allusions, became religious-prone.
Yet, we were able to atone.
Then, he mentioned their visit
to the Creation Museum,
and I truly became concerned.
He fondly related that at their retirement home
they had living to the left of their apartment
a professor of the Old Testament,
and to their right a prof of the New.
More and more, global warming
was named by him a hoax, a fake,
until I responded to a particular silly collection
of past, wrong predictions.
Our grandchildren would bear the brunt
of his Christian-infused wrong beliefs.

Sadly, I no longer heard from him.
I cannot help but grieve
having lost such a long-time friend
to ignorance and doctrinaire belief.

In times of rapid change,
experience could be your worst enemy.
John Paul Getty

Almighty

A German shepherd, a doberman
and a cat died and went to Heaven.
God asked the German shepherd
"How did you relate with your master?"
The German shepherd said
"I protected my master very well,"
and God told him "Here, sit to my right."
God asked the doberman
"And how did you fare with your master?"
And the doberman answered
"I loved my master very much,
and he loved me back."
And God told him "Go, sit to my left."
Then God asked the cat
"And how did you get along with your master?"
And the cat said
"Get off my seat!"

Truth in matters of religion,
is simply the opinion that has survived.
Oscar Wilde

Simone Biles

I like her face of steely resolve,
her body all muscle,
trained through and through.
And, of course,
to make her accomplishments possible,
her mind is a powerhouse, too.

There was no great genius
without some touch of madness.
Lucius Annaeus Seneca

155

Filigrane

Over the Bradshaws the full Moon rose.
Obscured a bit by trees in front
she ever so slowly crept higher.
But before she gained her freedom
in the heavens, clear,
She was marked by, what I call,
a lovely filigrane of twigs, I suppose,
imprinted on the Moon's disc,
ever changing in her slow traverse.
At times, a faint local breeze
caused the filigrane to momentarily flutter,
to cease.
While this all took place in slow motion,
at its equator the Earth travels
at a thousand miles per hour.

The external mystery of the world
is its comprehensibility.
Albert Einstein

The Presence

Don't be concerned about
what I am going to write.
It isn't that I am losing my mind.
There are times when I seem to sense
standing next to me a shadowy presence.
An entity of vague human shape,
silent, unmoving, its presence opaque.
I wonder what it is that I project?
Is it a guardian to protect,
or a reminder that my days in this world
are circumspect,
and in the not too distant future
will be checked.

Real knowledge is to know the extent
of one's ignorance.
Confucius

Bobcats

Our yards are crossed
by all kinds of creatures,
deer, javelina, roadrunners, quail,
skunks, coyotes, and bobcats, as well.
There may be quite a few others, too,
about which we haven't the faintest clue.
Bob, a new neighbor from Michigan,
claimed to have seen a Bobcat around.
I gently pointed out to the man
that, "while you may call them Bobcats in Michigan,
in Arizona we call the critter a Robertcat,"
Confound it! That is that.

It is a capital mistake to theorize before one has data.
Insensibly one begins to twist facts to suit theories,
instead of theories to suit facts.
Arthur Conan Doyle

Glory

My barely four-year-old RikkiCat has a strong desire
to get out of her indoor habitat.
To be walked with a harness and leash restricts her reach.
There's always something beyond that she sees
on some rocks, in some bushes, or up a tree.
Yet I cannot follow her wherever she likes to go,
for we both aren't free.
I am no longer limber enough, far less than she.
There are big, dangerous creatures out in this world,
javelinas, coyotes, bobcats, and such.
If I let her wander outside on her own,
who knows what she may encounter
being at the wrong place at the wrong time?
It is my decision, my responsibility, too,
to provide my companion with a life of her own.
To keep her cooped up inside the house,
to a life lacking stimulation, without bounce?
Thus I decided to let her go,
outside that is, from where she comes back off and on
to say hello.
She now enjoys a life of richness and splendor,
of magnificence and beauty, but also of danger.

Her Life will be for as long as it lasts,
maybe just a few years.
But it will be lived in glory,
and I love her for this.

Under a government, which imprisons any unjustly,
the true place for a just man is also a prison.
Henry David Thoreau

Juxtaposition

There was this friend of Turkish descent,
We talked and walked for years without end.
Then came the day when he was on his way
to travel to Turkey, as he did, come May.
That's when I juxtaposed Trump,
he had voted for, with Erdogan, he despised,
asking him why he traveled
from one misgoverned country to another.
Was it that I compared the two
so much alike, so much askew?
Unable to reconcile this discrepancy
in his mind, his top he blew,
and never again did we talk and walk.
My sarcasm was too much for more talk.

I don't like principles. I prefer prejudices.
Oscar Wilde

Lady, again,

but I start with a gentleman.
So called by an ignorant newspaper-man,
who posted that this gentle-man
had just been released from jail
on ten thousand dollars bail.
Now, why call a jailbird a gentleman
when some misdemeanor landed him there?
When ruffians dominated the not too distant past,
and often the present, still,
a man of manners and kind behavior
was therefore called a gentle man.
And a woman of manners and good breeding
was given the honorific "lady."
Otherwise she might be called a wench.
In the Anglo-Saxon world it has been forgotten that
all ladies are women, but not all women are ladies!
Behold, I have been called "Chauvinist" by a woman
for making this distinction.
Yet, I once drove down a winding road
when I saw a car in a ditch,
and stomping around was a foul-cursing woman
I'd rather call a bitch.

I considered assistance, but then let it go,
a lady she was not by a far stone's throw.
Another time, in Recovery, I returned to the world
from an anesthetic dream.
So pleasant it was to regain consciousness
when, next to me, a female voice erupted
in a most foul language stream.
Still dazed I asked the checking nurse
"Why does this woman so badly curse?"
She said that some people return to the world
from their narcosis, their minds rather stirred.
I rather think that this woman displayed
what truly in her mind was held.
A lady she couldn't be by any means,
she rather revealed her true routines.

Language is the dress of thought.
Samuel Johnson

Tweets

I never will be a Facebook guy
nor am I apt to "Twitter."
I'd rather meet my friends face-to-face, like to read,
or listen to real birds twitter in the trees.
What these days comes across,
especially from politicos,
is all too often lacking manners,
or is some kind of dross.
Does it really bring the world together
or is it, like most human matter,
most of the time just mindless chatter?
I know what I "like,"
don't need confirmation from the rabble,
which, come to think, is just so much babble.
It appears that this means of communication
has opened the doors for altercation,
all kinds of manipulation,
and ever less cogitation.

It is better to keep your mouth closed
and let people think you are a fool
than to open it and remove all doubt.
Mark Twain

Water

On one of the boulders in my yard
stands a water basin,
replenished daily by the irrigation system.
I watch my "clients" coming by:
a bobcat, chipmunks, quail, a roadrunner,
and many other birds, not to forget deer,
who cautiously drink upon coming near.
And, I suppose, then, in the dark, coyotes,
bandit-masked and black-and-white critters
leave their mark.
For javelinas it is out of reach.
It is a joy to watch them come,
to drink their fill, then quickly run.

Vision is the art of seeing the invisible.
Jonathan Swift

Ramblers

Some people like to ramble.
They talk of inconsequential things,
or a book they read, a movie they saw.
Do they love to hear themselves speak?
Is it attention they seek?
Or is their sense of awareness weak?

In der Kürze liegt die Würze.
In brevity lies spice.
German maxim

Hype

---

exaggerates
and ever more pervading
distracts from possible truth.
Can this be called uncouth?

Questions show the mind's range,
and answers its subtlety.
Joseph Joubert

Equanimity

Oh, equanimity, I keep striving for.
But might it be a quality, if so desired,
entering the mind on its own,
little by little, more and more?
At times it is challenged,
calling for awareness and calm,
an ongoing process, mental balm.
To be composed in the face of emotion and pain,
be conscious of reality's transience,
free of niggling little stuff,
and extend to all life compassion and love.
To be at peace with oneself and the world.

One's only failure is failing to live up
to one's own possibilities.
Abraham Maslow

Savior

The world needs saving
from champions of chaos,
such as Trump, the Brexiteers, Duarte, Bolsonaro,
Erdogan, Orbån, and more.
There is a surfeit of such people in power,
voted in by the ignorance of their constituents,
or is it that they saw them as saviors
of the troubles they beheld?
Today's world is faced with
bioengineering, artificial intelligence,
global warming and immigration,
calling for a unified stance.
But what to the world is being delivered
is nothing but official self-interest
with the big questions left to chance.
So, let's "pray" for this globe's ignorant, big and small,
who keep our world on its downward thrall.

Life begins on the other side of despair,
Jean Paul Sartre

Babble

Of the many human idiosyncrasies
there's the one of individuals
who love to hear themselves talk.
On and on it goes about things
from which the listeners, after awhile,
gladly away would walk.
The subjects may be important to the speaker
as such, but their content
does not convey very much.
Babble it becomes, the talker unaware
of why he or she is blowing that much air.
But the question remains:
"Why do they love to hear themselves talk?"
Does it make them feel important?
Are they looking for respect or admiration?
Or is plain ignorance at work?

To listen closely and reply well is the highest perfection
we are able to attain in the art of conversation.
François de La Rochefoucauld

Tit-For-Tat

When he gives a Tit,
he expects a Tat,
even reminds you
so that you don't forget.
I'd rather Tit,
never minding a Tat.
It is so much nicer
and that's a fact.

We know our friends by their defects
rather than by their merits.
William Somerset Maugham

Foibles

I love to mock this human trait,
the many foibles which are our fate.
Most are minor and personal flaws.
Others, more general,
can get stuck in your craw.
Thus I enjoy in some of my prose
to tease and to taunt,
knowing full well
that I'm part of the crowd.

The true mystery of the world is the visible,
not the invisible.
Oscar Wilde

Fallacy

We should put the erroneous belief to rest
that voters are the ones who always know best.
A number of examples across the globe,
such as the US of A, Brazil, Italy,
the Philippines, and the UK,
have demonstrated mindless decay.
To rationally pursue the questions posed
by our modern world, requires more
than for what the "average Joe" is prepared.
Even the ones supposed to be in-the-know
are lost in today's crazed puppet show.

Justice without force and force without justice
are both terrible.
Joseph Joubert

Captive

We are all captives
of the world we've created,
Some less, others more.
There are the fictions
of the society we live in,
there are also our very own.
For fictions they are,
there is no doubt.
Our minds are the most powerful tools
and give us, humankind, our clout
to control the world
more than we properly ought.

Ritual is a bulwark against chaos in the spirit.
Poul Anderson

Dharma,

---

the path I must follow,
the duties I must fulfill.
This is what Krishna,
the Hindu god of compassion,
tenderness, and love tries to instill.
It took me some time
to realize what all it was,.
And I'm working on it
for as long as I can.
Yes, I will.

A work is perfectly finished only
when nothing can be added
and nothing taken away.
Joseph Joubert

Impermanence

The Christians hope for Heaven.
The failed ones wish their spirit to live on.
The believers in rebirth
think to another life to return.
All stories created to overcome
the terror of impermanence.
Consciousness be damned!
As if one life lived were not enough!
Fill it to the hilt,
as much as you can.
Whatever you are able to.
And at last, simply be done.

Where there is no imagination
there is no horror.
Arthur Conan Doyle

Probabilistic

Neither am I a theist who believes in God,
considering His existence as true,
which many people would swear to know,
nor an atheist
denying His existence as fraud.
Both cannot know from observation
what is truly true,
but are forever beholden
by whatever story they were told.
Nothing in the world we know
can ever be totally certain,
only probably so.
Thus I'm content to live
with this smidgen of uncertainty
of a deity's existence
and the knowledge of the universe
at its today's veriest,
making me a probabilistic atheist.

I have never wished to cater to the crowd;
for what I know they do not approve,
and what they approve I do not know.
Epicurus

177

Freedom,

the power to think and act as one wants,
not being dominated by an external power,
nor imprisoned or enslaved.
Yet we submit to rituals aplenty
which take away the freedom
of any cognoscenti.
Rituals, to me, have always been a threat,
trying to pull me into a net,
an unwanted mindset.
I'm aware of their civilization's worth, their binding force,
but I prefer my very own course.
And yet, and yet,
there's always this Tao thought:
"When the Tao is lost there is Goodness,
When Goodness is lost there is Kindness,
When Kindness is lost there is Justice,
When Justice is lost there is Ritual.
Ritual is the Husk of Faith and Hope
and the Beginning of Chaos."

What is necessary to change a person
is to change his awareness of himself.
Abraham Maslow

Vision

No, not a vision of what may come,
nor an hallucination, come and gone,
but it's my eyesight that's slipping, another age-related conundrum.
Aside from the common floaters,
double vision, macular degeneration, astigmatism and glaucoma,
I now have a right-eye retinal trauma.
I see the front of approaching cars contorted.
Center lines on roads, too, have bumps facing right.
And any straight line my left eye sees straight,
while the right sees bumps which will not fade.
My proximal vision has turned to pits,
making my favorite pastime, reading, a pain to maintain.
Thus I am watching more TV
and worry how my driver's license
in a couple of years will turn out to be.
For driving, more attention is required.
Of great help are the routines acquired
in fifty-six years motoring accident-free.
I must yet see.
My freedom of movement is at stake.

Youth is a wonderful thing.
What a crime to waste it on children.
George Bernard Shaw

Loner

For much of my life a loner I have been,
an introvert, a spiritual nonconformist,
an outsider, whatever that means.
From my early years I've felt
that somehow I didn't fit in,
and, come to think of it,
had no desire to give it a spin.
What early on did drive me on
was to be my very own man.
I think I succeeded,
and when I look at my recent pics,
I am content with what they depict.

Alas, after a certain age every man is responsible for his face.
Albert Camus

The length of your education is less important
than its breadth, and the length of your life
is less important than its depth.
Marilyn vos Savant

Euphemisms

I find them objectionable.
And there are plenty.
"Why not call a "spade a spade?"
or "beat around the bush?"
As if "she passed away,"
instead of "she died,"
makes the subject of death,
the fear of it, more light.
But maybe it does?
Death, the end of consciousness,
is just too scary a cause.

The end of the human race will be that
it will eventually die of civilization.
Ralph Waldo Emerson

Climate Change

There are two kinds of deniers of climate change
the extreme ones even calling it a hoax.
Ignorant they are, don't know the facts,
and happily are stuck in a box.
Then there is the most troubling sort,
agreeing that change is taking place.
But they deny that the change is due
to man's excessive production of CO_2.
They are good at producing anecdotal facts,
but reject the findings many scientists back.
The latter seem to be intent
to make Armageddon, the Day of Judgment, come true.
I rather hold it with the Norse
whose Ragnarok the end of the universe meant,
even the gods would come to their end.
Anyway, they all are only stories
on which man's fantasy is spent.
But the facts of climate change are there
for anyone of sane mind to see,
except that human stupidity prevents too many – yet –
to see the forest for the trees.

Men are moved by two levers only: fear and self-interest.
Napoleon I

Integrity

One aspect of integrity
is to stand by what one has said.
Thus, when the statement is obscure,
to truthfully explain,
not refusing to answer instead.
To be honest and accountable
avoiding the other to remain ignorant
or be mislead.

The man who listens to reason is lost:
reason enslaves all whose minds are not strong enough
to master her.
George Bernard Shaw

Preposterous

In this universe so vast
billions of galaxies are amassed,
each again home to billions of stars.
Some may have planets similar to Earth;
some may bear life,
on some, civilizations may thrive.
On some, creatures similar to us may wonder
what this universe yonder is all about,
and have produced their own stories
of creation, morals, wars, and blunders.
Will one of their stories also talk about sin,
and how to deal with this evil djinn?
Might the goddess of their belief
dispatch one of her daughters to provide relief?
Will the fatherly Christian God
dispatch to these other places another one of His Sons?
Another son born by a virgin
to redeem these creatures of their postulated sins?
Goodness gracious,
how preposterous this is.

Life is just one damned thing after another.
Elbert Hubbard

Flame

Dancing and leaping
she resembles a flame.
Her thirst for life all-consuming;
intensity is her name.
Beware, you mortal, crossing her path,
she takes what she needs,
yet gives plenty in behalf.
Such beings, fiery and rare,
most richly humanness they share.
Then, touch this flame if you so dare.
If given the chance for one such to meet
drink most deeply,
while you can,
for your lifeblood is at stake,
and find how much you are able to bear.
Then, of it be forever aware
and relish how much you were able to share.

A flame that burns twice as bright burns half as long.
Laoze

Glimpse

You may wonder how I can write what I did
in my poem "Flame"
without having experienced
something similar or the same?
Well, twice I met such human females,
and got a faint idea of what it means.
Both, though, lacked the greatness
described in Flame.

Life is the art of drawing sufficient conclusions
from insufficient premises.
Samuel Butler

Orchid Man

One way or another I have collected
a goodly dozen orchid plants.
Some I bought, some came as gifts,
others were given to my care
to get them to bloom again
for their beauty to share.
They adorn the sills of my windows,
but are spilling over to other places now.
On some I observe how their air roots strain
toward moisture or water they'd like to attain.
Others firmly grip the rims of the vases,
like they anchor themselves to branches
high up in the tropical air.
And once they bloom
they will do so for weeks,
sometimes for months.
These plants, their flowers,
are for keeps.

Happiness lies in the joy of achievement
and the thrill of creative effort.
Franklin D. Roosevelt

Abomination

There is this man at the head of a country
who cheats, lies, distorts, abrogates, destroys,
brags, abuses and demeans, and whatever other
immoral behavior is his.
Then there are people who follow him.
What is one to make of them?
Is it not that by condoning his reign,
they become part of his immoral behavior
and guilty of the very same?
But they aren't aware of this,
or have no shame.

Only strong personalities can endure history,
the weak ones are extinguished by it.
Friedrich Nietzsche

Freedom 2

I have arrived at this point of my life
where I can say,
without circumlocution and decor,
what I think,
nothing less, nothing more.
And should some of this
not be to the recipient's mood,
well, then I give it a resounding hoot.

I'm old enough to know better
but I'm still too young to care.
Ogden Nash

Sin

Let's leave the original meaning behind,
"A transgression of the law of God,"
and stick with the term,
"To commit an offense or fault."
Then, the only sin there is,
is the sin of stupidity
when one ought to know better,
or better not be caught.

There is no sin except stupidity.
Oscar Wilde

Infallible

No, I'm not talking here of the Pope,
but rather ordinary people
who think they are incapable
of making mistakes,
those, who in their youth
their self-assurance,
ignorance, or both,
are too sure and thus beyond hope.
Then, when they least expect it,
and the shoe is dropped,
belatedly they will find out
that they have after all flopped.

Errare humanum est.
Seneca

Charm

Every once in a while
one sees on TV
a beautiful young woman,
not an actress,
just a human being,
maybe narrating, performing a musical piece,
whatever activity is hers.
Thereby she gracefully expresses her feminine charm
with a certain child-like demeanor,
in a lithe, adult physique.
A sensual delight it is
and also knowing me to be
a member of this human species.

Style is a simple way of saying complicated things.
Jean Cocteau

Rationalizing

Yeah, this is the game
everybody plays without shame.
To explain or justify what one has done,
has said oneself, or someone else.
What a waste of reason,
good mind, logic, plausibility is this,
when it would be saner to face just what is.

Beware lest you lose the substance
by grasping at the shadow.
Aesop

Sights and Sounds

Clouds drifting across the sky,
a rainbow rising high, a motorcycle's noisy roar,
a pair of turkey vultures soar, a phone ringing next door,
the song of birds, my cat's meow,
the scent of falling rain, a starry night,
the day's breaking light, the bark of dogs,
a distant fire engine's wail,
wispy contrails of a plane,
a lunch date to share,
cavorting in the sky a raven pair,
two bucks passing through the yard,
the setting sun a glorious reward,
wind whooshing through trees, the buzz of bees,
wind chimes tinkling, the laugh of a woman
on the street with others mingling.
Sights and sounds, ephemeral memoirs,
just as all loves and sorrows are.

... and on the pedestal these words appear:
My name is Ozymandias, King of Kings,
Look at my works ye Mighty, and despair!
Nothing beside remains. Round the decay
of that colossal wreck, boundless and bare
the lone and level sands stretch far away.
Percy Shelly

194

Besserwisser

Some folks cannot leave a statement be,
they fast respond with of what they are fond,
Kahneman's Fast Thinking,
never giving it time to think beyond,
about that which was stated,
reality be damned.
In American parlance,
this is no farce,
this German term is known as
smart-ass.

Even things that are true can be proved.
Oscar Wilde

Stimulation

Life thrives on stimulation.
Yet, when the mental fires burn low,
and all too often they do,
internal stimulation, creative thought,
self-entertainment,
is replaced by external foment,
input from the outside.
In old age it may consist
of eating and watching TV.
When people "play" with their smart-phones
they derive greater stimulation from
their electronic devices than from their
human partners.
Just observe a couple in a restaurant
facing each other,
playing their smart-phones!
Wherefrom do they obtain the more inciting
stimulation?
Or is it that the gismo won't argue, talk back?

All human beings should try to learn before they die
what they are running from, and to, and why.
James Thurber

Protest

Since 1 "lost" my wife,
the love of my life,
although there was a time
when 1 cast away reason and rhyme,
so, now, to protest life's pitiless score,
1 don't make my bed no more.

If you don't have time to do it right
you must have time to do it over.
Anonymous

But I don't.
H.W.

Personality

Rikki, my cat, has plenty of it.
Yet this does not make her a person.
Something doesn't fit.
Supposedly, a person has the capacity to reason,
of morality, and consciousness,
and is a member of a social relationship,
has legal rights and responsibilities.
Once more, something just won't fit,
for some of the above do not apply
to a certain president, a loathsome twit.
I'd rather reason with my cat
who can learn and behave
without morality and self-consciousness.
And that is that!

To know when to be generous and when firm –
that is wisdom.
Elbert Hubbard

Anthropocene

Ages ago, in little bands,
like other creatures
we wandered the lands.
Eventually, after the cold Pleistocene,
came the more clement present Holocene.
Now, that we are plundering the planet,
the anthropocene has been proposed,
the human-caused epoch,
one of the most calamitous times
this planet has ever seen.
There have been worse,
like Snowball Earth,
but what is happening now is our doing.
We are responsible
for our success or demise.

Some of our weaknesses are born in us,
others are the result of education;
it is a question which of the two gives us most trouble.
Johann Wolfgang von Goethe

Lupper

We have this combination
of breakfast and lunch
commonly known as brunch.
So, why not tie together
the other two,
lunch and supper,
as an early lupper?
It might reduce by quite a bit
the intake of too much fodder
and let people sleep
a heck of a lot better.

Good sense about trivialities is better
than nonsense about things that matter.
Max Beerbohm

Pursuable Entity

There is this young lady
of three-score-and-ten years,
slender, of good face,
and a demeanor to please.
Too bad she's not free,
so this is a tease.
If I were younger, unencumbered,
in good health, and without blight,
well, I'd give it a shot,
just for good company and what not,
and here and there a hug and a squeeze,
if that's alright.
All this, provided she too would agree,
she'd sure be a pursuable entity.

You should always say much more than you mean,
and always mean much more than you say.
Oscar Wilde

Irreconcilability

----

exists, when a wife believes
that her husband loves her
when all signs ought to tell her
that he does not.
When a creationist believes
the Earth is only 6000 years of age,
when the findings tell
that it is 4.5 billion years old.
When a person keeps rooting for Donald Trump,
when insight should be his
to see what a loathsome creature Trump is.
Such people reconcile the irreconcilable.
Even when two beliefs conflict,
reality is denied,
and harmony does not exist.

The opposite of a correct statement is a false statement.
The opposite of a profound truth
may well be another profound truth.
Niels Bohr

Rationality

Operating in accordance with reason or logic.
In January of 2018 stress got the better of me.
Confusion about my health
temporarily drained my rationality.
Then, in October of that year
low hemoglobin made me go to the E.R..
Upon checking in,
I had to fight tears to overcome
my physical and mental infirmity
to maintain rationality
a most precious commodity.

You'll live.
Only the best get killed.
Charles de Gaulle

Believing

The need and ability to believe
rests on the suspension of ratio.
Belief follows a different directive,
independent of reason.
This enables humans to believe
in the most improbable
or contradicting imaginations
and to maintain dichotomous
images in parallel.
Never mind that all beliefs, stories,
are man-made anyway.

You can change your faith without changing gods.
And vice versa,
Stanislaw Jerzy Lec

Autonomy

To do as we please
by what's morally right.
To be free of addictions
freedom's blight.
To follow the heart
through upsets and slights
into what's certain,
our eventual twilight.

Everything that irritates us about others
can lead us to an understanding of ourselves.
Carl Gustav Jung

Aberration 2

Provided there is no cataclysmic event,
hunky-dory we expect the world to tend.
Yet, in the Year-of-our-Lord
two-thousand-nineteen,
the monsoon was the poorest
we, for a long time have seen.
What's more of a puzzle
is the absence of insects,
not that I complain about this dearth.
Yet I wonder whether the two are connected:
the scarcity of insects
and the shortfall of monsoon.

The cure for boredom is curiosity.
There is no cure for curiosity.
Dorothy Parker

Tribalism

The other day
among some conservative friends,
I somewhat facetiously suggested that,
with all the star-spangled banners
displayed in the neighborhood,
including at our host's domicile,
I thought of hoisting the German flag,
down the street, at my pad.
Dead silence greeted my odious remark,
intended to raise the question
of overt demonstration of loyalty,
of patriotism, and not to forget,
of tribalism being a part.

Man is born free
and everywhere he is in chains.
Jean-Jaques Rousseau

Chaos

Ancient Greek philosophers thought
of the world as ordered – cosmos.
Today we have entered a world of chaos.
Disorder reigns, confusion is obvious.
Old orders are questioned, have run their course.
Many old and new social
and techno-scientific developments
have made living together on a global scale worse.
The ignorance at the U.S. presidency,
is only the tip of the iceberg.
The bewilderment is universal, of course.
We stand at the cusp
of two directions, two states.
With all that we know now,
if we rise to the challenge,
there is this choice of two fates,
one is downfall,
the other greatness.
More or less,
the dregs or the mind of the universe.

Man only likes to count his troubles,
but he does not count his joys.
Fyodor Mikhallovich Dostoyevsky

Clarity of Mind

I am of that age when some faculties fade.
Around me age mates, too, degrade,
their mental faculties slipping,
worse, Alzheimer's being their fate.
But I have vowed to fight
for the clarity of my mind.
A year ago when my hemoglobin
had dropped too low,
I, at the E.R., tearfully struggled to maintain
the clarity of my mind,
a taste of what age on some bestows.
But what concerns me even more
is the everyday task, the daily chore,
to make oneself think straight and clear,
a discipline of thought
without which writing turns to naught.
When I think what's arriving by email at times
too often erratic, unchecked, confused,
I cannot help but being little amused.

We Are what we think.
All that we are arises with our thoughts.
With our thoughts we make the world.
Buddha

Dream

Again and again, the dream recurs,
to leave the hubbub
of the contemporary world.
But not quite yet,
there's still much to be observed.
It being early September,
the mosquitoes have taken a break.
To sit in peace by the shore
of a small Canadian lake.
Gaze across its placid waters,
dusk settling at a rising moon.
The shimmer of its light,
a silver spoon.
A single-malt Scotch, neat,
its bouquet, not only, a pleasant treat.
A good friend nearby
with whom to trade a kind word, by and by.
Listening to the silence
and the haunting calls of a loon.

Life is one long process of getting tired.
Samuel Butler

Discipline

Of which there is many a kind,
but the one I refer to here
is the orderly, not prescribed,
conduct of behavior,
the self-control of the mind.

Self discipline is that which, next to virtue,
truly and essentially, raises one man above another.
Joseph Addison

211

Speaking One's Mind

I am of that age
when some things matter less,
others, like truth, do more.
What have I got to lose?
Thus I'm speaking my mind,
about what, I don't care,
or in what matters I've failed,
it is only fair.

Truth is a precious commodity.
That's why I use it so sparingly.
Mark Twain

Sui Generis

Rational to a high degree,
which is why I claim to be sui generis.

Very few of us are what we seem.
Agatha Christie

Three African Stories

The Lure of Africa   Page:
Zambezi
Tanzania Redux

There was a Time

when I walked the land,
my mate behind,
our cub on her arm.
I carry a club and check the wind,
for vultures circling means there may be a kill.
The savanna's grasses are high at this time,
hyenas or lions could hide nearby.
For me, down here, it is hard to tell,
but carnivore reek is easy to smell.
Vulnerable we are, out here in the open,
few acacias offer a quick retreat.
But we must cross this expanse
to the black line not far,
to find succor across in bushes and trees.
I must find water and food
for my cub and mate.
But the time's not yet right
to ponder my fate.

The surest way to be deceived
is to consider oneself cleverer than others.
Francois de La Rochefoucauld

Africa

I have been to the deserts,
the Namib, the Sahara.
I've canoed the Zambezi,
crossed the plain of Amboseli.
Ballooned the Mara, chased hippos in that river,
had elephants chasing me in Botswana.
Seen ancient ruins most plentiful, in Morocco, Libya, and Egypt.
Entered the Valley of Kings and Hatshepsut's temple
with my buddy, the only visitors there.
I have walked the bush in tow of a guide,
his rifle at the ready,
always wondering what the next thicket might hide.
I've seen giraffes, antelopes, crocs,
warthogs and lions galore,
elephants, buffalo, and many more,
seen them by daylight and in the night.
I've met and enjoyed many people from near and afar.
Believe me, dear reader,
when I hold it dear and say here:
"There's always the call of Africa."

The goal of life
is to make your heartbeat match the beat of the universe,
to match your nature with Nature.
Joseph Campbell

The Lure of Africa

Written in 2011

As of today, I have made seven trips to Africa and have written travelogues of several. It being highly unlikely that I will be off on an eight's venture, allow me to travel back in time, more than five decades, to write about my first trip to the 'Dark Continent.' Since childhood, when I began to read, and was fascinated by the German colonial exploits in east and southwest Africa, this continent exerted a peculiar fascination on me.

When I had reached 19, having traveled a bit in Germany and twice to Sweden, with my life unsettled, not knowing where to go, I hit on the idea of bicycling solo around the globe. My parents vetoed this thought. Then I came up with buying a motorcycle, attach a side car to it, find a companion, and travel from Germany via north and east Africa to Cape Town, there to hire on on a steamer to return home, but it took more than 20 years for me to eventually, make it to that city. Back then, I saved and saved my salary for this venture and sold all kinds of things to my colleagues in the design department I was working at, eventually acquiring about 3,000 deutschmarks. I found an age-mate to join me and eventually purchased that motorcycle rig. A solid hinged steel lid with a padlock covered the opening of the sidecar to protect our travel gear; the intention was for us to ride on the cycle back-to- back. A 20 liter gasoline tank was strapped to the outside.

A few days after my 20th birthday, the beginning of October 1956, we set off me after a week's earlier extraction of a molar. We headed south and stopped at the D.K.W. factory for a refurbishing of my vehicle, and had to spend more than had been budgeted. We did not carry cold-weather clothing and on our drive through the Alps, even through northern Italy, we came close to freeze our derrieres off. Oh, what a relief it was when, at last, we exited a road tunnel that opened to the warm breezes of the Mediterranean Sea. Down the 'boot' we drove, along the Amalfi coast to Naples, where we boarded an Italian steamer to take us to Tripoli in Libya. This was when King Idris still governed there, which makes me 'older' than Colonel Gaddafi, the usurper.

On the ship, we quickly became friends with a group of four, an about 30 year old German with his French wife, and their two, about 22 year old German

218

raveling companions, all riding in a small Fiat car. The couple was, as they old, on their way to accept the inheritance of a Kenyan farm. Arriving in Tripoli n the afternoon, we made every effort to get out of the city into open country where we could camp. Alas, the date palm groves stretched east for mile after nile, and we had to camp off the road in a palm grove. Shacks nearby caused us five males to share guard duty through the night. One of the two younger ellows picked up and ate the dropping dates – and suffered from – you know what – all the way to Cairo.

The road along north Africa to Cairo is paved all the way. Eventually, we eached the desert – not a sand dune desert – but one that, at least where it approached the coast, was covered by a low shrubby growth. Often, the oad stretched straight to the horizon. Sometimes we cut the brush as padding for our tent, as we did not carry air mattresses to save weight. Nevertheless, by trip's end the bottom of my tent resembled a sieve caused by ock punctures. Small stores along the road's about 1,500 miles afforded us to eplenish food supplies, also gasoline and water. We quickly took to an air-dried, salt and paprika-covered lean beef, called *pastorma*, to fry up. When, one time, we felt like scrambled eggs with fried *pastorma*, we – joy over joy – came across some kids selling baskets of small eggs beside the road by a village. We bought all of them. At camp that night, after frying some *pastorma*, cracked the first egg – and half of it plopped into the frying pan. They had all been cooked for preservation!

n many places along the road the earth was covered by reflecting splinters – glass – a remainder of the north African war. And it rained in northern Africa, at east in the fall. There were days when we got soaked in the morning, only to have air-dried again by afternoon.

Camel herds crossing the desert, had to be watched for, since these creatures often stopped short of the road, only to step onto it, just prior to our arrival at that spot, a potentially deadly event. We all had visas for Egypt, and when we entered this country, lying farther south, we enjoyed the warmth we had missed. With no sun screen available at the time, just plain Nivea cream, the skin of our noses came off in sheets.

Eventually, we entered the chaos that was Cairo and somehow learned of a lodging place for foreigners, run by German Lutheran Sisters! We found acceptance there and, through the following days explored the city, where we got to know an elderly Jewish couple at a market place – yes, there were still Jews living in Egypt at the time – who invited us for dinner. I felt honored being German! But we never made it to the Egyptian Museum, since, a few days after our arrival, Britain, France and Israel attacked Egypt because of Nasser's expropriation of the Suez Canal. For at least ten days we were now stuck at our place of residence. It had become too dangerous for us foreigners to venture into the city. We occupied a small room on the roof of the multistory building and from there were able to watch the air raids of the attackers outside the city.

Prior to the attack, new people had arrived at our place, among them a German girl in her early twenties, who appeared quite naive to us even younger, but by several days more experienced travelers. We cautioned her to wash all fruit with potassium-permanganate, the only means available to us to sterilize fresh produce. She proudly told us the next day that she had washed also some sesame seed-covered bread sticks in such a solution. And to top it off, she went out for dinner with a dashing Egyptian army officer, against our warning. A young German fellow showed up with red pustules all over his body. He had been an overnight guest in a bedouin's tent and had become the victim of bed bugs. Two, a bit older German globe trotters claimed to have been the models for a German author's trilogy of former P.O.Ws, who escaped, traveled the world. I had read the three books and, from what recalled, their exploits sounded true.

The food at our lodging place consisted in a large part of rice, of which we quickly grew tired, longing for fried potatoes that were served only once a week. One day I splurged to sneak to a German restaurant, where delighted in a square meal of sausages with sauerkraut and mashed potatoes. Already in Libya we had grown tired of the Arab flatbread, like pita bread, and were happy when we found small breads Italian-style Libya having been an Italian colony, where this kind of bread had been introduced. Later, in Cairo, it was interesting to watch delivery boys in the morning, transporting huge trays of this flat bread, which, fresh from the oven hadn't flattened yet, but was round, almost like balloons. We also fixed ourselves between meals a helping of fried *pastorma* with scrambled eggs and – shame on us – followed local custom and tossed the egg shells off our rooftop abode, down onto the street. Yes, there was some danger walking

220